THE MUSIC
OF AFRICA

J. H. KWABENA NKETIA

W · W · *Norton & Company · Inc* NEW YORK

Acknowledgements

Photographs found on the following pages have been supplied by
the owners or custodians, whose courtesy is gratefully acknowledged:

Kwesi Andoh, Institute of African Studies, Ghana: pp. 22, 37, 62,
71 (left), 73, 74, 75, 80, 87, 88 (bottom), 93, 96 (top), 100, 101
(top), 103, 105 (top), 113, 212.

Photo HOA-QUI: pp. 31, 59, 78, 96 (bottom left), 101 (bottom),
105 (bottom), 106 (top), 114, 207, 227 (all three), jacket.

Ghana Information Services: p. 47.

Hermann, Paris: p. 71 (top right).

Horniman Museum, London, S.E. 23: p. 71 (bottom right).

Halifax Photo: pp. 88 (top left), 95

Kenya Information Service: pp. 90, 106 (bottom).

Photo C. DUVELLE: p. 96 (bottom right).

UNESCO: p. 101 (middle).

E. J. Brill, Leiden: p. 8.

Library of Congress Cataloging in Publication Data

Nketia, J H Kwabena
The music of Africa.

"Selected discography": p.
Bibliography: p.
1. Music, African—History and criticism.   2. Music—
Africa—History and criticism.   I. Title.
ML350.N595M9   780'.96   74-4178
ISBN 0-393-02177-7
ISBN 0-393-09249-6 (pbk)

This book was designed by Andrea Clark.
Typefaces used are Janson and Centaur.
Set and printed by Vail-Ballou Press, Inc.

Printed in the United States of America

1   2   3   4   5   6   7   8   9   0

TO DR. EPHRAIM AMU

who did so much
for African music study

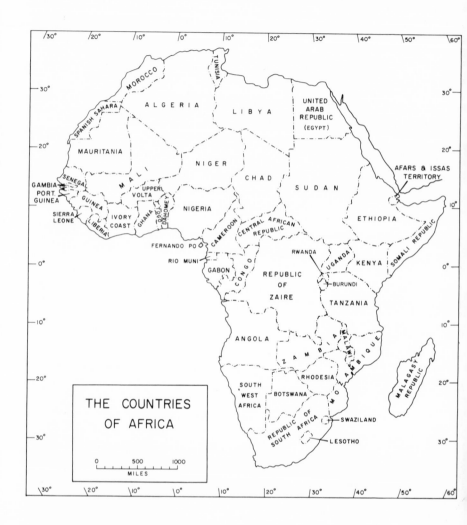

THE COUNTRIES

OF AFRICA

0   500   1000

MILES

Contents

Preface

THIS volume has been designed as an introduction to the music of Africa for the general reader and the college student. It attempts to provide a broad survey of the musical traditions of Africa with respect to their historical, social, and cultural backgrounds, as well as an approach to musical organization, musical practice, and significant aspects of style. These are discussed and interpreted in the light of the data now available in the form of recordings, monographs, and periodical articles, in addition to my own experience with this music in different parts of Africa.

Because of the extensive range of indigenous musical resources found in Africa as a whole, it has been necessary to consider not only the documented features that the various traditions have in common, but also those aspects of specific cultures that are significant or that appear to constitute appreciable extensions of general principles. The study of African music is at once a study of unity and diversity, and this is what makes it exciting and challenging.

This study is presented in the form of a series of analytical observations with appropriate illustrations. These illustrations have, however, been kept to a minimum, since it is possible to overload a work of this nature with an array of ethnographic and related data drawn from a wide variety of ethnic traditions that nevertheless do not add significantly to the text. For those interested in such data or in the study of the music of single societies, of single countries, or of particular instruments, I would call attention to the relevant sources listed in L. J. P. Gaskin's *A Select Bibliography of Music in Africa* and A. Merriam's *African Music on L.P.: An Annotated Discography*.

It is important that the reader who is not familiar with the countries of Africa and the ethnic groups whose names appear in the literature on Africa become acquainted with these as quickly as possible, since this unfamiliarity is likely to slow down his reading. To help those who do not have this background, geographic locations have been provided along with references to African peoples in the text of this study so that they can be identified on the maps provided.

I cannot conclude without expressing my gratitude to those who encouraged me to write this book or gave me the opportunity to work on parts of it by inviting me to write or lecture on aspects of the music of Africa. I would like to mention in particular the Department of Music and the Institute of Ethnomusicology of the University of California at Los Angeles, where I have been teaching regularly since 1968, and the Music Department of Harvard University, where I lectured for a semester as the Horatio Appleton Lamb Visiting Professor of Music. To Mr. Nissio S. Fiagbedzi, author of *Sogbadzi Songs—A Study of Yewe Music*, I owe special thanks for his invaluable aid in transcribing the Ewe texts. To my colleagues, clerks, and field assistants in the Institute of African Studies of the University of Ghana, I owe a special debt of gratitude.

J. H. KWABENA NKETIA

Legon, Ghana

SECTION ONE / *The Social and Cultural Background*

1 / The Musical Traditions of Africa

IT is now common knowledge that the continent of Africa is not as culturally homogeneous as has been generally assumed. North Africa is inhabited by societies whose languages and cultures are very closely related to those of the Arab world of the Middle East, while the southern portion is dominated by settler populations from Europe.[1]

By extension, the music practiced by these societies belongs to stylistic families outside Africa. Arabic music is cultivated by societies in north Africa, as well as by Arabs or Arabized communities in northern Sudan, parts of the Maghreb, and the east African littoral. Although the music of these cultures appears to have developed some characteristics of its own on the African continent, it belongs to the Oriental family of modal music. Its classical, folk, and popular idioms are so distinct from those of the rest of Africa that it cannot, on stylistic grounds, be included in the family of indigenous African music. Likewise, those varieties of Western music cultivated in the southern portion of the continent by Euro-

---

[1] North Africa includes the Arab states of Morocco, Algeria, Tunisia, Libya, and the Republic of Egypt; northern Mauretania and the northern part of Sudan share in the culture of this area. Southern Africa includes the Republic of South Africa, Southwest Africa (Namibia), Rhodesia (Zimbabwe), and Lesotho, Swaziland, Botswana, and Malawi.

pean settler populations and by Africans of Western orientation must also be excluded from this family of musical styles.

When we turn to the rest of Africa, we find African societies whose musical cultures not only have their historical roots in the soil of Africa, but which also form a network of distinct yet related traditions which overlap in certain aspects of style, practice, or usage, and share common features of internal pattern, basic procedure, and contextual similarities. These related musical traditions constitute a family distinct from those of the West or the Orient in their areas of emphasis.

The most important characteristic of this family of musical traditions is the diversity of expressions it accommodates, a diversity arising from different applications of common procedures and usages. In part, this may be the outcome of the complex historical grouping of African peoples into societies ranging from as few as two thousand people to as many as fifteen million. Over seven hundred distinct languages are spoken by these societies; and although these languages can be grouped into large families,[2] in some cases many hundreds of years separate the members of such families from their parent languages. The counterpart of this linguistic situation exists in music, for the music of Africa, like its language, is, so to speak, "ethnic-bound." Each society practices its own variant. Hence one can speak of the Yoruba variety of African music, the Akan, the Ewe, the Senufo, or the Nyamwezi variety, and so on.

The Historical Perspective

Several factors account for this diversity of musical traditions. The environmental conditions under which African societies evolved have by no means been uniform, nor have their histories followed the same course. The cultures of those who occupy the savannah and grassland areas have tended to differ from those

---

[2] See J. H. Greenberg, *Studies in African Linguistic Classification* (New Haven, 1955), or *The Languages of Africa* (Bloomington, 1966).

whose countryside is predominantly of the tropical forest type. There are likewise riverine people as opposed to highland dwellers, as in the past there were predominantly agricultural peoples, pastoralists, and others who combined both of these occupations. Small pockets of hunters and gatherers—notably the Pygmies of central Africa and the Bushmen of the Kalahari Desert—also appear to have sustained this mode of life.[3]

Most of these societies also engaged in other pursuits—in trade, light industries such as weaving and pottery, and the making of wooden, gold, iron, or bronze artifacts, with the choice of medium generally related to environmental factors. Variations in the cultural patterns of societies placed in such circumstances were inevitable, and these were reflected not only in their social and religious institutions and material cultures, but also in their arts, which now constitute the heritage of modern Africa.

The cultural differences tended to be perpetuated by the kinds of political units into which African peoples traditionally grouped themselves. Until recently, most African societies lived as distinct political units—some as societies without centralized political institutions, and others as societies with state systems.[4] Many of the latter had flourished in ancient times, and some emerged as kingdoms and empires of considerable magnitude in different historical epochs. In west Africa,[5] for example, the kingdoms of Ghana, Mali, Songhai, and Kanem-Bornu flourished one after the other in the Sudanic belt, to be followed by the growth of forest states such as those of the Yoruba, Benin, Dahomey, and Ashanti.[6]

---

[3] See G. P. Murdock, *Africa, Its Peoples and Their Cultural History* (New York, 1959), 48–63.

[4] See Simon and Phoebe Ottenberg, eds., *Cultures and Societies of Africa* (New York, 1960).

[5] West Africa refers to the stretch of land from Senegal to Lake Chad. The countries of this region from west to east are Mauretania, Senegal, Gambia, Mali, Guinea, Sierra Leone, Liberia, Ivory Coast, Ghana, Upper Volta, Niger, Togo, Dahomey, Nigeria, and the Cameroon. The coastal belt of this area is often referred to as the Guinea Coast, while the savannah belt is identified as the Sudanic area.

[6] For a brief general introduction to African history, see Roland Oliver and J. D. Fage, *A Short History of Africa* (Harmonsworth, 1962). For west Africa, see A. A. Boahen, *Topics in West African History* (London, 1966), or G. T. Stride and C. Ifeka, eds., *Peoples and Empires of West Africa* (London, 1971).

Over forty such indigenous states existed up to the end of the colonial era.[7] Some of them underwent drastic changes under colonial regimes, but many of them have continued to flourish—generally in a modified form—within the framework of modern African states. In colonial times there were, as there are now, societies like those of the Nuer of southern Sudan or the Akan of Ghana, who shared common cultures but who traditionally grouped themselves into different political units. On the other hand, there were also single states that embraced peoples of different ethnic groups.

Population movement that followed territorial expansion, wars, famine, and other crises drove wedges into homogeneous groups and gave rise to mixed populations. Sometimes branches of one group migrated to another location, thus splintering the group: for example, the Sandawe, an offshoot of the so-called click-speaking peoples of southern Africa, now live in Tanzania.

The establishment of territorial boundaries during the nineteenth century ignored the composition of the indigenous population, introducing similar complications. For example, in eastern Africa, the Luo are found in both Kenya and Tanzania, while members of the so-called cattle-culture complex are scattered throughout Uganda, Kenya, Sudan, and Somalia.

Cultural Interaction

Although all these groups retained their identity, they did not live in isolation. In the pursuit of trade, members of some societies, such as the Mande and Hausa, traveled far and wide; other states maintained diplomatic relations with one another. Likewise, there was cultural interaction that resulted in the borrowing and adaptation of cultural items, including music.

As a result of this interchange, there sometimes occur musical types bearing the same names in different areas, as well as other

[7] The colonial era, also known as the European period, dates from the sixteenth century to 1960.

types with different names but similar patterns. For example, *asafo* music of warrior organizations or one of its subtypes, *as ɔnkɔ*, *kyirem*, or *apagya*, will be found in the Akan, Ga, Adangme, and Ewe areas of Ghana; in Dagomba country in Ghana, a music and dance type called *kanbonwaa* is modeled on the same kind of music, but combines both Akan and Dagomba musical styles. Similarly, a musical style called *jongo* is found among many societies in northern Ghana—in Frafra, Kusasi, Kassena-Nankani, Builsa, and Sisala—while *damba* is performed in Dagomba, Gonja, and Wala at festivals of Islamic origin. The use of similar musical patterns or terms extends beyond regional boundaries: for example, the Dahomean musical genres *kete, ketehoun, katanto,* and *akofin* are reminiscent of some types also prevalent in the Akan region of Ghana.[8]

The areas of intensive interaction tend to follow fairly well-defined geographical boundaries which incorporate centers of economic or religious activities. One such area extends from the western Sudan to Lake Chad and its environs, where varieties of instruments of the lute and harp-lute family and certain features of monodic (single-voice) singing style predominate. Another such area is eastern Africa, including the East Horn (Somalia and Ethiopia), which is set apart from west Africa by a similarity of instrumental types. Varieties of long trumpets, zithers, lyres, harps, and kettle drums link a number of ethnic groups in this area.[9]

The distribution of types of instruments and even of musical features in more extensive areas also suggests that the musical cultures of African societies were not isolated, but overlapped and interacted. The use of xylophones, for example, extends right across the continent, from east to west through the Niger-Congo linguistic zone. A map of the distribution of this instrument prepared by Olga Boone has been revised by A. M. Jones, who has superimposed on it the distribution of thirds (see map, p. 8), since

---

[8] See J. H. Nketia, "History and the Organisation of Music in West Africa," in *Essays on Music and History in Africa*, ed. K. P. Wachsmann (Evanston, 1971), 3–25.

[9] See K. P. Wachsmann, "Musical Instruments in the Kiganda Tradition and Their Place in the East African Scene," in *Essays on Music and History in Africa* (Evanston, 1971), 93–134.

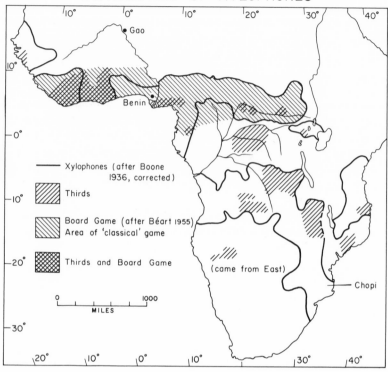

DISTRIBUTION OF XYLOPHONES

Xylophones (after Boone
1936, corrected)

Thirds

Board Game (after Béart 1955)
Area of 'classical' game

Thirds and Board Game

(came from East)

Gao

Benin

Chopi

0   1000
MILES

it seems to be concentrated in the same zone.[10] Another illustration is J. Vansina's survey of the incidence of welded double-flange bells in the area of the Niger-Congo divide, which suggests not only that the societies in this area interacted, but also that there was probably a common model, followed by societies in this zone, of state organization in which such bells functioned as part of the regalia of kings.[11]

[10] A. M. Jones, *Africa and Indonesia* (Leiden, 1964), 123. The "thirds" referred to on the map describe the interval most commonly used in two-part singing (see p. 161).

[11] J. Vansina, "The Bells of Kings," *Journal of African History*, X/2 (1969), 187–97.

Contact with External Cultures: the Legacy of Islam

The political and cultural evolution of interacting indigenous states did not follow an even course. In addition to internal factors that affected their progress, there were also external factors that influenced the direction of their development. Africa had trade connections with countries of the Mediterranean and the Near East, as well as with Southeast Asia. References to Africa in Indian and Chinese manuscripts show that in the precolonial era there were trade connections with these countries as well.

The societies of Africa that interacted with peoples of other lands included those of

a. the East Horn (Somalia and Ethiopia), whose proximity to the civilizations of Egypt and the Mediterranean as well as Arabia is reflected in its cultures and ethnic composition;

b. eastern Africa, where Arab traders were active and penetrated the interior as far as the Congo, and where Afro-Arabic interaction was so strong that it stimulated the growth and spread of Swahili as a *lingua franca;*

c. the island of Malagassy, the scene of Malayan, Indonesian, and African interaction; and

d. the Sudanic belt of west Africa, which interacted with Islamic north Africa.

The impact of Islamic and Arabic cultures had a far-reaching influence on many of the cultures of all these areas, and particularly on those of the savannah belt of west Africa, the coastal belt of eastern Africa, and Sudan. Pockets of non-Islamized groups remained within these areas, while those that embraced Islam varied in the extent to which their cultures were transformed.

The rise of an Islamic ruling caste and the formation of Islamic states were features of this period of African history.[12] Such states

---

[12] The Islamic period of African history began in A.D. 741 with the conquest of Egypt. Islam became firmly established on the north African littoral by the end of the sixteenth century, and continued to penetrate sub-Saharan Africa until the nineteenth century.

were formed in some cases (such as the East Horn) by Arab settlers, and in other cases (such as northern Nigeria) by leaders of African societies who had embraced Islam and who felt committed to wage holy wars in order to subjugate the indigenous populations under the political rule of Islam. The potentates of such states adopted the regalia of sultans, and some Arabic musical instruments, particularly aerophones and drums, became a regular feature of their court music.

The effect of the transplantation of Islamic and Arabic cultures on the musical traditions of African societies was, however, uneven. While some regions (such as northern Sudan and the Mediterranean littoral, occupied by bedouin Arabs who interacted with Berbers) adopted Arabic musical traits, other areas underwent varying degrees of adjustment to the impact of Arabic music. The adjustments, however, were not as radical in most parts of sub-Saharan Africa as it is generally supposed. In some parts of west Africa for example, it appears that African converts to Islam did not have to abandon their traditional music completely, even where they learned Islamic cantillation or became familiar with Arabic music. On the contrary, they continued to practice it, making such modifications in resources or refinements in style as contact with the new musical culture suggested.

The resources drawn upon by societies in contact with Islamic and Arabic cultures lay primarily in the field of musical instruments (see p. 97). A few varieties of closed and open drums were borrowed as additions to local forms, or for use in special contexts. Some lutes, reed pipes, and long trumpets were similarly adopted and integrated into local musical cultures.

Generally, the Arabic types simply provided the models for the manufacture of local equivalents. Hence some instruments, like the one-string fiddle, show variations in size and shapes, as well as timbre. Similarly adopted plucked lutes come in different sizes and have different kinds of resonators: some have round resonators, while others have rectangular forms. Only because such instruments could be made with local materials, unlike Western instruments, could they be adapted for local use.

Sometimes not only the instruments were adopted, but also the terms for instruments (e.g., *tabale, bendair, ghaita*) and customs associated with particular musical instruments.[13] The diffusion of these elements did not always take place through the adoption of Islam. The normal processes of cultural interaction permitted those not in direct contact with Islam to borrow from their Islamized neighbors, or from contact agents (those who carry cultural elements from one group to another) such as Mande and Hausa Muslims, who habitually traded in their areas.

It must be emphasized that the interchange between African and Arabic cultures did not benefit only Africa. As Henry G. Farmer points out, there is "some evidence of Moorish indebtedness to the western Sudan." [14] In the field of music, the adoption of the African drum *ganga* in north Africa is a noteworthy example of reciprocal borrowing. Secondly, it was not only Africa that benefited musically from Islamic civilization. Curt Sachs tells us that

> Nearly all the musical instruments of medieval Europe came from Asia, either from the southeast through Byzantium, or from the Islamic empire through North Africa, or from the northeast along the Baltic Coast. The direct heritage from Greece and Rome seems to have been rather insignificant, and the lyre is the only instrument that might possibly be considered European in origin.[15]

Making a similar comment on the musical instruments of the Orient, Sachs writes, "Islamic influence has left a quantity of traces on Southeast Asia, but most Islamic instruments have been absorbed by primitive tribes and have no place in art music, with the exception of the Persian *spike fiddle*.[16]

Apart from instrumental resources, it was generally only the more superficial aspects of Arabic musical style that seemed to have attracted those societies in contact with Islam who did not give up their traditional music. These traits include features of

[13] See Helen E. Hause, "Terms for Musical Instruments in the Sudanic Languages: A Lexicographical Inquiry," *Journal of the American Oriental Society*, Supplement 7 (1948), 1–73.

[14] Henry G. Farmer, "Early References to Music in the Western Sudan," *Journal of the Royal Asiatic Society* (1939), 577–78; and Helen Hause, "Terms for Musical Instruments," 23.

[15] Curt Sachs, *The History of Musical Instruments* (New York, 1940), 260.

[16] Ibid., 242.

vocal technique identified with Islamic cantillation—such as voice projection and its accompanying mannerism of cupping the ear with the palm of the hand, or a slight degree of ornamentation—and facilitated by the traditional emphasis in Islamized areas of Africa on monodic singing. The more important aspect of Arabic style, the system of melodic and rhythmic modes, does not seem to have been generally adopted, for this would have entirely changed the character of the music of those societies.

Moreover, there was much in Arabic musical culture to reinforce traditional African musical practice, for

> Music accompanied the Arab from the cradle to the grave, from lullaby to elegy. Every moment of his life seems to have had its particular music—joy and sorrow, work and play, battle-throng and religious exercise. . . . Vocal music has always been more keenly appreciated by the Arabs than the purely instrumental music. Their ardent taste for poetry determined this to some extent, although the pressure of legal opinion which frowned on instrumental music *per se* also contributes to the preference. . . . There were also instrumental pieces, but far oftener they were used as preludes or interludes to vocal items.[17]

It must be noted also that some of the basic elements of African cultures survived the Islamic impact and thus reinforced the practice of music associated with social customs. As J. S. Trimingham points out,

> When Islam is adopted the community does not suddenly change its social pattern but remains a unity distinguished by its own pattern of custom. In time Islam becomes closely intertwined with communal life, yet without disintegrating its basic structure. Only when a Muslim family is compared with a pagan family belonging to the same social group can the effect of Islam be seen. New features are superimposed, but basic customs, the composition of the extended family, the authority of its head, the rules of succession are little affected.[18]

It is not surprising, therefore, to find extensions of traditional customs or the use of indigenous resources in the musical practice

[17] Henry G. Farmer, "Music," in *The Legacy of Islam*, ed. Sir Thomas Arnold and Alfred Guillaume (London, 1931), 358–59.
[18] J. Spencer Trimingham, *Islam in West Africa* (Oxford, 1959), 125.

of Islamic-African communities. As Trimingham further observes, "the musical aptitude of the African, characterised by the chant, highly developed rhythm and antiphony, has found expression in the recitals of religious poems in Arabic and vernaculars at *dhikr* gatherings."[19] Nor is it strange to find residual elements of African vocal style coloring African renditions of Islamic cantillations.[20]

Some Islamic communities set the context of Islamic worship and other religious and social occasions apart musically. According to Akin Euba, the Yoruba Islamic community uses "orthodox Arabic Music" during worship, but performs traditional Yoruba music for social activities as well as Muslim festivals.[21] It is noteworthy that in some societies, Muslim musicians perform not only for their own religious community, but also for other social groups and non-Muslim festivals and ceremonies as well. It is no doubt this practice of integrating Muslim and non-Muslim activities within the single community that has facilitated the integration of Arabic and indigenous musical resources in the traditional music of Islamized African communities.

The Legacy of Europe

No less far-reaching was the contact with Europe established through trade, Christianity, and colonial rule, for this set in motion new forces in acculturation that have helped to reshape Africa. The grouping of indigenous African societies and states within new territorial framework which began in this era continues to be the basis of modern African states.[22] Thus Nigeria, the largest African country, with a population of over fifty million, is inhabited by the

[19] Ibid.

[20] See Lois Anderson, "The Interrelation of African and Arab Music. Some Preliminary Considerations," in *Essays on Music and History in Africa*, ed. K. P. Wachsmann (Evanston, 1971), 143–70.

[21] Akin Euba, "Islamic Musical Culture among the Yoruba: A Preliminary Survey," in *Essays on Music and History in Africa*, ed. K. P. Wachsmann, 171–81.

[22] The basis for the partition of Africa was agreed upon by the European colonial powers at a conference held in Berlin in 1884.

Yoruba, the Hausa, the Nupe, the Tiv, the Ibo, the Efik, the Ijaw, and several other African societies, each of them in a different region of the country. Likewise, Ghana, a small country with a population of some eight million people, is made up of several ethnic groups who formerly lived as independent entities. All of them have continued to maintain their cultural identity within the framework of the state. A similar picture exists in east Africa: Uganda has twenty-five ethnic divisions made up of Bantus, Nilotes, and Nilo-Hamitic peoples, while Tanzania has over one hundred thirteen distinct groups.

One of the problems facing modern African states, therefore, is how to integrate the societies politically and culturally within their state framework. The question of African unity has also loomed large in the politics of modern Africa. Efforts have been made by the Organization of African Unity to set up machinery for the promotion of inter-territorial cooperation in the arts and for the organization of pan-African festivals through which greater cultural integration can be fostered on a continent-wide basis.

It was not only political change that contact with Europe generated, but economic change as well. Indigenous trade was promoted by the new demands of foreign traders. The slave trade, for example, flourished and paved the way for the transplantation and growth of African and African-derived music in the New World. The traditional emphasis in agriculture was transformed from mere subsistence to the cultivation of cash crops, while markets were created for the sale of European goods. As the economy grew, Western instruments originally introduced through the church and the military became available in shops for the few adventurous musicians who were willing to play them. The adoption of the Western guitar by traditional musicians in some parts of Africa followed this general trend.

All these developments were encouraged and strengthened by the activities of the church, which preached against African cultural practices while promoting Western cultural values and usages. It adopted a hostile attitude to African music, especially to drumming, because this was associated with what seemed to Christian evangelists "pagan" practices. Moreover, this music did not appear to be suitable for the form of Christian worship that Westerners were accustomed to. The fact that drums and other percussion instruments were used in the Ethiopian church, which had been established in the fourth century A.D.—much earlier than any other church in Africa—did not affect the evangelistic prejudices. In some areas the converts were not only prohibited from performing traditional African music, but even from watching it. Hence, active participation in community events—in festivals and ceremonies—was discouraged.

Because indigenous African music could not be used, the substitution of Western music was vigorously pursued. Some churches translated Western hymns into African languages and thus made them a little more meaningful to their converts. The music curriculum of Western-style education introduced by those churches emphasized Western hymns, school music, and art music.[23] This pattern of education reached its peak when the tradition of preparing African students for British examinations in music was established. In 1933, the Education Department of the Gold Coast (Ghana), for example, was able to make the following announcement in the local *Teachers' Journal:*

> The Associated Board has just opened its examination to West Africa. The local secretary is Mr. W. E. F. Ward, Achimota, who will provide on application free copies of the syllabus and full details of the examination etc. At a small charge, he will also supply specimen papers, copies of prescribed music and other matter. For the present only written examinations will be held, the papers being set and marked in England. Practical examinations will be held in future if there are enough candidates to justify the Board in sending an examiner from England—but not for a year or two. Nevertheless these examinations are easily the best in the Gold Coast, and there are no better examinations available anywhere. They provide a regular, carefully graded course to the highest level: and they should be a means of

[23] A compilation of tunes set to Twi words and arranged for male voices for use by students of the Presbyterian Training College (Akropong, Ghana), for example, included excerpts from the works of Haydn, Handel, Bach, Mozart, Beethoven, Mendelssohn, and Brahms, while many Bach chorals were incorporated into the hymn book.

improving the musicianship of the teachers and pupils of West Africa.[24]

It is noteworthy that almost one hundred years before this advertisement, Ghanaians were being taught to play Western music so that they could entertain those who lived in the European forts and castles. In his work on *Ashantee and the Gold Coast* (1841), Beecham observes that "the musical taste of the people is evidenced by the native band at Cape Coast Castle which plays admirably by ear, several of the most popular English tunes." [25] The need for providing Western musical entertainment for colonial officials and traders was met subsequently by the army and police bands, to which Africans were recruited and trained by Western band conductors. Before the attainment of independence, it was these bands that entertained people at the European clubs and played for the garden parties held by governors of the colonies.

The effect of transplanting Western music into Africa in the aforesaid manner was threefold. First, the continuity of traditional music in its unadulterated form outside the adopted Western institutions was unintentionally assured by the exclusion of traditional musicians and their music from the church and educational institutions, the most direct sources of Western musical influence. Most of the traditional political, social, and cultural institutions that supported traditional music flourished in spite of the presence of Christianity, Western cultural institutions, and colonialism.

Second, the exclusion of those who were systematically exposed to Western culture from participation in traditional music led to the emergence of new "communities of taste," identified with varieties of Western music. These communities still exist in independent Africa, for the legacy of Europe is inextricably bound in with the cultures of contemporary Africa.

Third, the creative urge of members of these new musical communities found outlet in new compositions. These have been developing in two streams. One is that of modern popular music, which appears in different forms on the African continent and

[24] *Teachers' Journal*, V (1933), 230.
[25] John Beecham, *Ashantee and the Gold Coast* (London, 1841), 169.

takes its place alongside Western popular music in the cafe, the night club, the ballroom, and other places of entertainment. Well-known forms of this music are the *highlife* of west Africa, the *kwella* of South Africa, and the popular music of the Congo. Each of these functions as a musical type consisting of percussion, set rhythmic and melodic characteristics shared by individual items in its repertoire, and, of course, Western-derived harmonies. The other stream includes new forms of art music designed for the church, educational institutions, and the concert hall. It includes music for Western-type choirs (which often sing in four-part harmony), as well as instrumental music. However, choral music seems to have received much more emphasis, owing to its early development in the Christian Church.

These new forms of composition were originally based entirely on Western models with which composers were familiar— hymns, anthems, marching songs, and so forth, set to local languages, and as instrumental pieces. However, with the gradual growth among the literate community of nationalism, which served to stimulate a new awareness of the African heritage of music, a few composers began to turn their attention to traditional African materials. Nevertheless, what emerged was not a complete break from Western tradition as they knew it, but its use for the creation of a new Western-derived African music—that is, music based on African melodic and rhythmic structures, but exploiting Western harmony and developmental techniques as well as employing both African and Western musical instruments.

This approach seemed welcome to some critics of the colonial period who saw the future of African music in terms of a synthesis of the resources of Africa and Europe. Concluding his essay on "Music in the Gold Coast," which appeared in the *Gold Coast Review*, W. E. Ward suggests that "if it could learn from Europe modern developments in form and harmony, African music should grow into an art more magnificent than the world has yet seen." [26]

[26] William E. Ward, "Music in the Gold Coast," *Gold Coast Review*, III/2 (1927), 223.

In a book review which appeared in *Overseas Education*, Reginald Foresythe further emphasized that

> African children should be taught African music alongside with European music. Only in this way can we expect to create an African school of composition, which will necessarily have to be a fusion of African and European idioms. Of course all this rests with individual genius, but I look forward to the day when great works by African composers, works stamped with that originality and depth that is Africa's will be heard in the concert halls of the world.[27]

These observers merely took notice of what Africa itself was doing within the context of acculturation. Present-day commentators, however, are ambivalent. Some recognize and encourage those new forms, which have become identified with non-traditional subcultures and urban social life. But purists decry them as hybrids and vestiges of the colonial past that must be discouraged; for whatever their merit in terms of satisfying a social need of the moment, they lack the stylistic diversity and vigor of traditional music. It seems, however, that nothing short of a cultural revolution can set the clock back, for this problem is not peculiar to the recent history of music in Africa. It is characteristic of the entire way of life of modern Africa, its institutions, and its creative arts—its literature in English, French, and African languages, its modern paintings, sculpture, and drama—all of which reflect the African heritage as well as various aspects of the legacy of Europe. That is why decolonization is regarded by those concerned with the African image as an important task facing independent Africa.

It is no wonder, therefore, that the search for African identity and the growing awareness of the cultural achievements of the past have awakened in independent Africa a new interest in traditional music. The Christian churches have begun to explore the resources of this music and to consider how Christian worship can be Africanized. The question of the adequate use of traditional music in African music education is likewise receiving attention, while traditional music is being featured in the programs of African radio

[27] Reginald Forsythe, review of William E. Ward's *Music: A Handbook for African Teachers* (London, 1939), in *Overseas Education*, XI/3 (1940), 174–75.

and television stations. The preservation, promotion, and re-creation of this music now forms part of the cultural policy of many African governments. Anniversary celebrations of independence and other national occasions give it a special place, while national dance companies highlight the heritage of traditional music and dance in their respective countries.

New Horizons

It will be evident from the foregoing brief survey that the factors that shape and maintain musical practice in Africa operate in the direction of both change and continuity. Some elements give rise to the widening of regions in which indigenous musical traditions overlap, while others lead to greater heterogeneity in details of style.

The Islamic period increased the scope of overlap to the extent that it introduced new resources and features that were adopted over an extensive area. But it also created a new cleavage between the musical practice of Islamized and non-Islamized societies. Within Islamized societies, continuity of tradition was assured through the integration of old and new materials and through the extension of the use of music in new aspects of social life.

The European period was marked by divergent tendencies that led to the emergence of new musical subcultures. It introduced new levels of identification that went beyond those of the ethnic group, and heralded a new era of internationalism. New distinctions in musical practice arose—particularly between traditional and contemporary practice, as well as in levels of musical activity relating to idiomatic categories—which established the division between traditional, popular, and art music in sub-Saharan Africa.

The complex nature of the musical scene was recognized during the post-independence period. Much of what was inherited from the colonial period was retained, including Western military band music, and even national anthems in Western musical idiom were accepted. Now it appears that increased attention is being given to expanding the scope of traditional music in national programs, in addition to emphasizing its relevance to modern cultural institutions. The creative response to all this is beginning to show itself in adaptations of traditional music for use in new contexts, as well as in new popular and art music based almost entirely on traditional materials.

A knowledge of traditional African music in its social context is, therefore, a prerequisite both for understanding the contemporary musical scene in Africa and for gaining some insight into the musical experience as it relates to the African in his personal and social life. In the chapters that follow, we shall examine the characteristics of this music with respect to its contextual relations (using the community as a frame of reference), the range of instrumental and vocal resources evident in the specializations of societies that practice this music, the varieties of structures and procedures that are utilized in traditional musical expressions, and various aspects of performance.

2 / *Music in Community Life*

In traditional African societies, music making is generally organized as a social event. Public performances, therefore, take place on social occasions—that is, on occasions when members of a group or a community come together for the enjoyment of leisure, for recreational activities, or for the performance of a rite, ceremony, festival, or any kind of collective activity, such as building bridges, clearing paths, going on a search party, or putting out fires—activities that, in industrialized societies, might be assigned to specialized agencies.

Those who get together in such communal activities generally belong to the same ethnic or linguistic group. The basis of association for music making, however, is usually the community, those members of the ethnic group who share a common habitat (such as a group of homesteads, a village, a town, or a section of a town) and who live some kind of corporate life based on common institutions, common local traditions, and common beliefs and values.

The degree of social cohesion in such communities is usually very strong. Not only may the members know one another, but they may also be bound by a network of social relations: they may be kinsmen or members of social groups that cut across kinship.

Spontaneous response to group needs and involvement in collective activity are generally expected of the members of a commu-

Expression of group sentiment: a state funeral procession accompanied by drums carried on the head.

nity. Organized games and sports (such as wrestling), beer parties and feasts, festivals, and social and religious ceremonies or rites that bring the members of a community together provide an important means of encouraging involvement in collective behavior, a means of strengthening the social bonds that bind them and the values that inspire their corporate life. The performance of music in such contexts, therefore, assumes a multiple role in relation to the community: it provides at once an opportunity for sharing in creative experience, for participating in music as a form of community experience, and for using music as an avenue for the expression of group sentiments.

The emphasis on community experience does not, of course, preclude individual music making by both young and old, especially when it is related to personal life and individual economic activities. Music can be performed by children, for example. Among the Fon of Dahomey, a child who loses his first tooth has to sing a special traditional song to commemorate the event.[1] When children assist in the economic activities of their parents or are given special responsibilities, such as looking after flocks, they may be encouraged to play flutes for their own enjoyment, for giving signals to their companions, or for guiding their flocks.

> Among the Brifor of Ghana, for example, shepherd boys make pipes out of the stalks of millet and play these to give signals to other shepherd boys, especially when they are taking cattle out in the morning to graze in the field. Builsa herders similarly play flutes to give signals to one another, particularly when returning home with their cattle.[2]

Music is also performed by individual adults, either for their own enjoyment or for the young. Cradle songs are typical examples of this: their texts may reflect not only themes interesting to a child or musical elements amusing to him, but also references of interest primarily to mothers and adult listeners. In addition to cradle songs, some societies make provision for a variety of domestic songs, or encourage the use of songs as an accompaniment to domestic activities. Grinding songs, pounding songs, and songs sung when the floor of a newly built house is being made have been noted; some of these, however, also take place as group activities.

Individual musical expressions have a place in traditionally masculine activities as well, and may be found in recreation, in work situations, or even in the context of worship. An instrumentalist may play for his own enjoyment—he may perform in the open without addressing himself to a specific audience, or he may perform in seclusion. The Konkomba lute player performs for himself only when he wants to keep in close communion with his god, as does the Gabon ritual expert who plays the *wombi* chordophone. The sight of the lonely wayfarer playing the *sansa* (hand piano) as he travels is not uncommon in some parts of east Africa, while shepherds are known to spend their time playing the flute. Such individual expressions become a part of the community experience only when they take place in social contexts. Accordingly, they may

[1] See M. J. Herskovits, *Dahomey*, Vol. I (Evanston, 1967), 275.
[2] J. H. Nketia, *The Sound Instruments of Ghana*, in preparation.

be encouraged or requested where they have something to communicate to an audience. Thus, the individual singing of dirges, praise songs, or boasting songs, and the performance of solo instrumental music that carries significant messages feature in the activities of some social occasions.

In general, however, community life lays much more emphasis on group musical activities than on solo performances. Many social occasions are dominated by the performance of a chorus of boys, girls, men, or women, by the singing of mixed choruses, or by performances of drum, xylophone, flute and trumpet, or chordophone ensembles, as well as mixed instrumental and vocal groups.

The Selection of Music

The actual music that may be performed on any occasion depends on the social event and those involved in it, for it is customary to organize the music in relation to the different phases of community life or in terms of the needs of special situations. These categories of music fall into two groups.

The first consists of musical pieces that are not conceived of in sets, but that may be unified by a common contextual reference. This would include the music performed on ritual or ceremonial occasions at prescribed stages of the proceedings—preceding, accompanying, or following prayers, speeches, ritual actions, or processsions. This music may not necessarily form a coherent formal unit or musical type.

The second class includes musical items that share common characteristics and are grouped in sets. Each such set of pieces generally constitutes a category of music or a distinctive musical type, and may be identified by a name, the choice of which may be guided by different considerations. For example, among the Akan of Ghana, a musical type may be named after those who perform it; thus, the music performed by hunters (*abɔfoɔ*) and warrior organizations (*asafo*) bear similar titles. But this is by no means the rule. A musical type may also be named after the function it performs; thus, a category of songs performed by women in time of war, when the men are away, is called *asrayere* ("visiting the wives"), for it is special music that brings the women together to wish their men well. These songs are also called *mmobomme*, songs of prayer for wishing a person well.

The social occasion on which a musical genre is usually performed or the activity, custom, rite, or festival with which it is associated may lend its name to the related music. Accordingly, the songs of puberty rite (*bragorɔ*) are called *bradwom* (*dwom* meaning song), while the music of *kundum* festival is similarly called *kundum*.

Sometimes a name, a proverbial saying that catches the fancy of a performing group, or the name of a person who originates a musical type may be used as a label for the music; this is particularly true of music performed for entertainment or recreation. Examples have been noted of labels such as *ntan* ("bluff"), *sika rebɛwu a, ɛpere* ("money struggles before it vanishes"), *onni bi amane* ("the suffering of the person who has no relations or friends").

The principal instruments used in a given musical type may also provide the name for the music. Thus the music of trumpets is given the same name as the trumpets themselves, *ntahera*, music in which the gourd stamping tube *adenkum* is the principal instrument is also known as *adenkum*, and music in which a box, *adaka*, is used as a substitute for a master drum takes a similar name, *adakam*.

When there is a specific name for the dance for which a musical genre is performed, this may also be used as a label for the music. Similarly, where dance items are intended for specific people, such as women of royal blood or porters of the royal court, the dances, and in turn the music, may be named after these categories of people.

It is not usual to provide names for individual items of a musical type, except where they constitute distinctive stylistic variants, or where it is necessary to refer to separate components specifically. This is particularly true of instrumental music, where each work may have a title that refers to its verbal basis, its style, the context of use, or mode of performance. Where instrumental items separated in this manner are combined with a chorus, each piece may belong to a set of songs and sometimes to a dance style.

Occasionally, one comes across musical types whose songs are grouped into subcategories on the basis of their themes, modes of performance, or contextual reference. The Adangme *klama*, for example, has a number of subcategories: *klama* for each of the principal cults, *klama* for the *tegble* heroic association, *klama* for puberty festivals, and proverbial and historical *klama* that may be sung in appropriate contexts. Similarly, the Akan dirge has subcategories for the different clans, particular lineages, members of *ntoro* groups, and specified individuals.

These various ways of naming and classifying musical genres demonstrate that the corpus of music practiced in an African community or in the wider society of which it is a part may have some kind of internal organization that groups items into sets, or relates items or groups of items to specific contexts.

Social Control

Implied in the internal organization of musical items and musical types is the exercise of some measure of social control. The music for a rite, a ceremony, or festival may not normally be performed in another context unless there is some special reason for doing so. On the same basis, the choice of musical resources—for example, the use of musical instruments—may be regulated: special drums not used elsewhere may be set aside for the worship of the divinities, while musical instruments dedicated to kings may not be played for ordinary individuals. Where the same instruments are used, the repertoire may be different.

Furthermore, the type of performance allowed for different occasions or situations may be controlled. The full ensemble may be used on one occasion and a smaller one for another. The periods for musical performances may likewise be regulated. The incidence of particular forms of music making may be related to leisure time, the ritual calendar, crises in the life of the individual or the community, and the exigencies of the seasons, in terms of which communities order their lives. There are communities that vary their emphasis on recreational music making relative to their agricultural activities, making it somewhat sporadic during the sowing season, but frequent and intense during the harvest season or during the dry season. There are others that respond to changes of the moon, and take advantage of moonlit nights for the enjoyment of music and dance as well as other recreational activities, such as story telling and games.

Sometimes the schedule of musical activities is related to the beliefs of a community—to the wishes of the gods they worship or to the reactions evoked from the spirits and forces that are believed to play a vital role in the drama of human existence. Among the Lele of Kasai, for example, rules about drums are enforced by religious sanctions. Drumming is a legitimate nighttime activity, and may occur in full daylight only on days of rest; during periods of mourning that may last up to three months, dance drums may not be beaten in this particular village.[3] Similarly, in Ga society, drumming is banned for three weeks before the annual harvest festival begins.

The implications of all this is that we should not expect to hear music in an African community every hour of the day or every day of the week, nor should we expect to hear music on every social occasion or during every kind of collective activity. African societies are selective: some of the rites performed in a given society may be musical events, while others are performed quietly with little or no music. Likewise, the singing of work songs may be a feature of only some types of manual labor. In this regard, African societies differ in the kinds of activities for which they provide music. Some societies, for example, celebrate marriage with a great deal of music, while others do not; similarly, some use music in the rites performed for twins, while others do not make these a focus for music making.

Scope of Musical Activities

The nature and scope of music making is generally related to the aims and purposes of a specific social event or to the needs of the performers. As in many cultures of the world, music making may be organized as a *concurrent* activity, that is, as incidental or

[3] Mary Douglas, "The Lele of Kasai," in *African Worlds*, ed. Daryll Forde (London, 1954), 1–26.

background music for other events such as games, wrestling matches, walking parties, processions, beer parties, and feasts. On the same basis, music may be related to the needs of performers in a variety of ways. It may be performed by street or market vendors to attract customers; by teams of fishermen as they row their boats or haul their nets; by agricultural, cooperative work groups; or, in certain societies, by selected musicians for the butchers and smiths, who apparently require music while they work, both for their own enjoyment and as a source of attraction and entertainment for their customers.

A vivid example of this use of music is given by Camara Laye in his story of *The African Child*. A woman comes into his father's workshop with a go-between, someone with a more-than-average command of the Malinke language. He is also versed in the artistic expression of the people, and can shower praises on the goldsmith and provide a musical background to the whole process of gold melting—a mysterious procedure, which commands an attitude of reverence on the part of the goldsmith as well as all others present. Laye writes:

> The praise singer would install himself in the workshop, tune up his cora, which is our harp, and would begin to sing my father's praises. This was always a great event for me. I would hear recalled the lofty deeds of my father's ancestors, and the names of these ancestors from earliest times. As the couplets were reeled off, it was like watching the growth of a great genealogical tree that spread its branches far and wide and flourished its boughs and twigs before my mind's eye. The harp played an accompaniment to this vast utterance of names, expanding it and punctuating it with notes that were soft, now shrill.[4]

Another kind of setting for the performer is found among the Frafra of northern Ghana. In this society, a player of the one-string fiddle and a rattle player accompany teams of men who cut grass. As they play, the workers swing their cutlasses in a concerted manner to the rhythms of their music, causing the slashing sounds of the blades to fall regularly on the main beats. This has a remark-

---

[4] Camara Laye, *The African Child*, (Glasgow, 1959), 23.

able effect on the speed as well as the efficiency of grass cutting, for rhythmic movements that are properly organized on some regular basis appear to be less fatiguing than movements in which exertion and release of effort do not form an ordered sequence. In some societies, the music is not as closely integrated with work as in this example, but is performed in the background. A. A. Njungu tells us that in Barotseland, "village men, on returning from the fields, usually gather under a big tree listening to one of them playing piece after piece of music on one of our several musical instruments, while the rest work at the various crafts." [5]

On ceremonial and ritual occasions, music making may similarly go hand in hand with set sequences of symbolic actions, performed with or without props by specified people playing given roles. These actions, which are dramatic in character, take place in the presence of some participants or spectators. Music may be integrated with the event, either to set the mood for the actions or to provide an outlet for expressing the feelings they generate. It may also be used to continue or heighten the dramatic action; hence, it may punctuate statements or prayers, or provide a continuous background of ordered sounds.

When a chief dies in Sukumaland, Tanzania, for example, some stages in the funeral are marked by music designed to perform various dramatic functions. The funeral announcement includes drumming, for the drums associated with the office of a chief (*ntemi*) can convey this message in a more forceful and dramatic manner to the community. According to Hans Cory, the big drums, *lugaya* or *milango*, are turned upside down soon after the death of the chief, when preparations for burial are made. While the corpse of the dead chief is being carried to the grave, the *itemelo* drum is beaten. All those who hear the sound of the drum understand; the word spreads: *ngoma ya chibuka*, the drum has burst— that is, the chief is dead.

For the installation of the new chief who succeeds a dead *ntemi*, a different kind of music is performed, and different stages of the ceremony are again marked by music. As soon as the new chief comes out of the door of the new palace, a song is sung by an office bearer:

> Kawahenja, you small and pretty bird,
> Come out that you may be seen by everybody.

A number of formal questions are put to him, and the end of each question is punctuated by drum beats. The chief and his retinue then mount a platform near a drum stand, and receive an ovation from the people. Silence is enjoined by drum beats as the chief is formally proclaimed. While war songs and dances are performed, the chief retires for a time, and then returns to the ceremonial ground. The ceremony reaches its musical climax when he returns. The names of the clans of his predecessors are recounted one by one, and each is punctuated by a drum beat. As each clan is called, the members dance forward to the chief, brandishing their spears as a sign of their loyalty, and then return to their places in the crowd.[6]

The second approach is to organize music as a *terminal* activity or as an activity preceding a major event. Thus in some societies, the use of musical sounds made for flushing animals from cover during hunting is differentiated from the music performed after the hunt. The final phase of a cermony or rite may be marked by music and dancing, which may be given more time than the actual ceremony or rite itself.

There is a great deal of emphasis in community life on music making as a terminal activity, for it is through such participation that a large number of people identify themselves with the aims and purposes of a social event and interact with one another. Enjoyment of the music of the occasion is always a paramount consideration; hence, music making in such contexts may be protracted.

A third way of organizing music is to make it a *free* activity, unrelated to a ritual, a ceremony, or any form of nonmusical event, for music and dancing constitute an important means of recreation in community life. This form of music activity, however, depends very largely on the musical interests of a community, as well as on the initiative and leadership of individuals.

---

[6] Hans Cory, *The Ntemi: The Traditional Rites in Connection with the Burial, Election, Enthronement and Magical Powers of a Sukuma Chief* (London, 1951), 10.

The Setting of Performances

Since the traditional approach to music making makes it a part
of the institutional life of a community, the physical setting for performances can be any spot suitable for collective activity. It may be
a public place, or a private area to which only those intimately concerned with the event are admitted; a regular place of worship,
such as a shrine, a sacred spot, a grove, a mausoleum; the courtyard of the house where a ceremony is taking place, or the area
behind it; the scene of communal labor, the corner of a street habitually used by social groups for music and dancing, a market place,
or a dance plaza.

Among the Sonjo of Tanzania, plazas are specifically constructed for such activity, both for religious festivals and dances,
and for secular singing and dancing. The religious plaza is situated
somewhere near the center of every Sonjo village. It consists of a
clearing large enough to hold several hundred dancers, with an
enclosure at one end for meetings of the village council. Behind the
enclosure is a thatched hut, which is used as a sanctuary. The floor

Music and dance in a village square

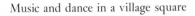

of the sacred dance plaza, the largest and most central in the village, is always well kept. In addition, every section of the town has a small plaza, built on the same pattern and used for recreational singing, dancing, or special ritual.

It is unusual to find permanent structures designed specifically for musical performances. On special occasions, however, temporary structures may be erected to provide shade for a limited number of guests and spectators; seats may even be provided as well. The general practice, however, is for everything to take place in the open air, and for the audience to stand around the performers or close to them.

Those who gravitate toward the performing arena are drawn to it for different reasons. Some may come out of curiosity or merely because they are attracted by the sound of music; others attend because they like the musical genre performed by the group. (It is rare for a performing group to specialize in a wide range of musical types; indeed, most groups limit themselves to just one or two musical types in addition to their repertoire of songs and instrumental styles. Those who come to watch and hear them may be familiar with their music, and may enjoy hearing what they already know, while listening to the creative variations that may be made in the course of the performance.) There are always some who attend for ethical or social reasons—to grace the occasion or give support to the performers because they are relations, neighbors, or members of the community, or because they are guests or patrons of the performing group. Others may attend because they are leaders of the community or ritual experts who have a function to perform.

These differences in motivation are reflected in the behavior of members of the audience. The attitude generally expected of them is not one of restrained contemplative behavior, but of outward, dramatic expression of feeling. Individuals may shout in appreciation when something in the performance strikes them, or indicate at a particular point their satisfaction with what they have just heard or seen. In addition, their conduct may indicate that the performance satisfies or makes manifest a social value, or that it satisfies a moral need. On the other hand, the audience's expressions may be negative at any given moment, indicating disapproval or even displeasure. For example, there are certain expectations that dancers must fulfill, and certain things that they must not do. They must not throw glances at people while dancing, for good dancers must be so deeply engrossed in what they are doing, and doing it so well, that people will notice it without the dancers' having to "catch their eyes." In addition, the Akan say that good dancers must not hold themselves "as erect as the stalk of a plantain."

Limited participation in the performance itself may be extended to the spectators. In some contexts, they may join the chorus; they may also enter the dancing ring either to dance or to give moral support to the dancers by placing coins on their foreheads or in their mouths, by placing pieces of cloth or kerchiefs around their necks, or by spreading pieces of cloth on the ground for them to step on. That is why dancing in the ring "as though she had no relations," no one to give her support or encouragement, is an expression of sadness for a woman in some societies.

Of course, the presence and participation of an audience influence the animation of a performance, the spontaneous selection of music, the range of textual improvisation, and other details; and this stimulus to creative activity is welcomed, and even sought, by the performers. A physically present audience, however, is not always necessary. Furthermore, even where an audience is present, it may not necessarily be the primary focus of attention, since a performance may well be for the benefit of someone who may not actually be present, or simply for the enjoyment of the performers.

Where an audience is present, there is usually not a wide gulf or a clear-cut boundary between them and the performers, except where the nature of the performance requires this. When the performers group themselves at one end of the arena, they are flanked on their left and right by the spectators in a horseshoe formation, taking care to leave enough space for the dance. Where instrumentalists and chorus take their places at the opposite ends of the arena, the spectators may line up on their left and right, forming a square but leaving an open space between the two groups for dancing. When the performers arrange themselves in a circle, the spectators similarly form a circle around them. The actual details of the seating or standing arrangements for the performers themselves vary in different societies. Whatever the formation, the atmosphere in the performing arena is usually informal, and spectators are free to move about or leave any time they wish.

On the whole, intimate indoor settings for musical performances are not as prevalent as outdoor settings. An indoor setting would generally be reserved for restricted audiences such as kings, patrons, and friends, or for a limited group of people involved in a private ritual or ceremony. Whatever the setting, the focus is on music making as a social activity, one that emphasizes artistic as well as social, political, and religious values. Music may be performed for the sheer fun of it, for the message that it communicates, or for the outlet that it provides for social interaction or the sharing of community sentiments; it may be performed as a tribute to an individual, an offering to a deity, or a service to a potentate. The approach to music making that links it to institutional life ensures spontaneous participation and identification with the musical life of a community.

3 / *Performing Groups and Their Music*

In African societies, participation in music may be a voluntary activity or an obligation imposed by one's membership in a social group. Such a social group may be a descent group (a group of people who trace their ancestry back to the same person), or it may be any group based on the broader societal classifications of age, sex, interest, or occupation. Where an African society is stratified, as, for example, the societies of the Hausa of Nigeria[1] and the Wolof of Senegambia,[2] musical activity may be related to class structure. In such societies, music making generally belongs to a social class of a low rank, and active participation usually takes place only on this level. The higher class is content to be entertained, or to leave the musical aspects of ritual and ceremonial occasions to professional musicians and others who assume musical roles in such contexts.

Spontaneous Groups

Two major types of performing groups need to be distinguished: those spontaneous or organized groups that are au-

[1] See M. G. Smith, "The Hausa System of Social Status," *Africa*, XXIX (1959), 248.
[2] See David P. Gamble, *The Wolof of Senegambia* (London, 1957), 44–45.

tonomous, and those that are attached to traditional establishments and are made up of musical specialists. The spontaneous music groups are formed when people who are not in associative relationship come together of their own accord to perform the music prescribed for a specific occasion. This music may be performed by only a section of the community—by children, men, or women. Hence a person's response to the performance needs of an occasion may be related to the musical roles associated with his primary biological group or to the nature of the occasion.

Thus children may perform in certain well-defined contexts; for example, the Ashanti song of insult for the habitual bed-wetter may be sung by other children at a special corrective ceremony. Similarly didactic songs form part of the circumcision rituals for boys in some parts of Tanzania, while boys undergoing circumcision rites among the Wolof of Senegambia are taught various songs in the evening while still at the camp waiting for their wounds to heal. Initiation songs for boys or girls are not uncommon in other societies. Other songs sung by children include those incorporated into stories or embodied in games—particularly counting or number games, language games, and games involving dancing or some other form of movement.

Similarly, there are songs performed by women during ceremonies and rituals that are the concern of women. In Akan society, for example, the puberty rite for girls is celebrated by women, and the songs and drum music for this occasion are accordingly performed by adult women. When one examines the texts of such songs, one understands why this is so, for they are not only songs of joy, but also songs in which references may be made to the duties and expectations of motherhood. Among the Adangme of Ghana, it is the women who supervise the elaborate *dipo* puberty institution and its ceremonies and music. The girls are kept for several weeks of instruction in mothercraft, in the special music and dancing of the transition rite, and in the customs and history of the society. They are put on a fattening diet so that they may look plump and beautiful on graduation day. Musical processions to ritual places, feasts in the home, singing and dancing parties, and a series of public activities mark the end of the training, at which time each girl is richly adorned with precious beads, gold or-

Women singing and accompanying themselves with rattles at a *dipo* puberty ceremony

naments, and ankle buzzers for the display of music and dancing in the market place. For several days afterward, the girls go round the town performing *dipo* puberty music and dance, and collecting gifts of money from those who watch them. Although the adolescent girls perform at the climax of the training period, most of the music of the public ceremony is executed by the adult women, sometimes with the support of a few male drummers when *klama* songs and dances are performed.

Responsibility for similar ceremonies or for ceremonies centering around little children is also assumed by women in other societies. The songs of the Sukuma of Tanzania for ceremonies celebrating twins, for example, are sung by adult women who perform the necessary ritual. According to Hans Cory, the songs of *ngoma ya mabasa*, as this musical category is called, are extremely indecent; and during the ceremonies, the language of the people in charge is purposely interspersed with obscenities. Only adult women are given this license.

Among some societies in eastern, central, and southern

Africa, rites for healing the sick or for correcting certain disorders are also performed by women who sing special songs and accompany themselves with rattles and drums.[3] Mention should also be made of the special musical role that women play at funerals. In some societies, it is their function to wail, with or without words, in choral laments as well as dirges sung individually. Some societies have dirges for particular lineages and clans, dirges for specified individuals, and dirges for royal lineages performed by the women members of the lineages, clans, or households of the deceased.[4]

Women play a special musical role at the courts of chiefs by virtue of their position as kinswomen, wives, or concubines. Among the Ankole of Uganda, for example, a king's future wives were traditionally taken care of by the widows of his brother who "taught them to dance, sing and play the harp" so that they might entertain the king when he visited them in the evenings.[5]

All the foregoing examples are sung by women by virtue of their sex and roles in society, and not necessarily because of their musical interests. This does not, of course, mean that they do not enjoy what they perform or even take pride in what they do; but there is a difference between the bonds that bind them together in such contexts and those that operate when they form permanent associations or "bands" of their own specifically for making music.

Just as there are musical roles ascribed to women, so are there roles that men may assume in certain contexts. There are situations in which these roles are played spontaneously by men who are not in any kind of associative or organized relationship: for instance, in societies where social life revolves around periodic brewing of millet or banana beer, drinking songs may be performed quite spontaneously. The performance of work songs by gangs of men or by cooperative work groups would seem to fall within this cate-

[3] For an account of this see Hans Cory, "Ngoma Ya Shetani: An East African Native Treatment for Psychological Disorders," *Journal of the Royal Anthropological Institute*, LVI (1936), 209.

[4] See J. H. Nketia, *Funeral Dirges of the Akan People* (Achimota, 1955).

[5] K. Oberg, "The Kingdom of Ankole in Uganda," in *African Political Systems*, ed. M. Fortes and E. E. Evans-Pritchard (London, 1940), 142.

gory, as would the singing of special songs by men during a funeral ceremony.

Sometimes situations are found in which all members of a community may join together in singing special songs of a ceremonial occasion, as in the ancestral rites of the Sambaa of Tanzania.[6] In the *fika ya ngoma* ceremony performed for a male relative one to four years after his death, for example, there is a preparatory rite in which a beer pot is used as the main ritual object. A hole is dug for burying this pot and the master of ceremonies sings as he digs. The participants outside the house where the ceremony is taking place approach it, singing, "Evil enters the house of the master." Those inside the house reply in song, "They come in, they go out"; that is, evil spirits may enter the house, but the ceremonies about to be performed will soon drive them out. Slender bunches of leaves and twigs of certain plants are hung over the pot, while the chanting continues. The master of ceremonies ties bells around both legs, singing:

> May I tie the string of ornaments of the master of
> ceremonies?
> Let us work to please him.

He starts to dance, taking small steps along the walls of the hut; other people join him, singing and dancing. This continues for about four hours. Shortly after this preparatory rite, the main ceremony of invocation of the major ancestral spirits and their appeasement is begun. The master of ceremonies begins to sing:

> Hear, hear you, the message of wisdom, you novice who
> came to worship his own spirit.
> Fall on your knees, worship *nkoma*, worship.
> God the spirit of Zeuta may sleep in peace, and that of
> Bangwe.[7]

The people then respond in chorus:

---

[6] Hans Cory, "Tambiko or Fika," *Tanganyika Notes and Records*, LVIII (1962), 274–82.

[7] *Nkoma* in Sambaa (the language spoken in Tanzania) means "skull." It is used here metaphorically for the ancestors whose spirits are being invoked at this ceremony. Zeuta and Bangwe are appelations for gods in Sambaa.

> Fall on your knees, worship *nkoma*.
> God the spirit of Zeuta may sleep in a deep sleep, and
>   that of Bangwe.

The master of ceremonies invokes his own spirits; after the last invocation, he begins to dance to the accompaniment of drums, bells,
and songs. Those present then join him in the dance around the
beer pot. After a while he takes off the bells and hands them over to
the clan elder, who then invokes the ancestral spirits of the clan one
by one, mentioning the name of the deceased for whom the ceremony has been organized last. When this particular person is mentioned, the drums are beaten and the women sound a loud, sharp
trill. After silence is restored, they all sing in a chorus:

> May the spirit sleep in peace.
> One grain of corn can fill the silo.

That is, provided the spirits do not interfere, one man is capable of
filling a house with his children. The master of ceremonies takes
over the bells. A live chicken is brought, and beer and a few beads
are forced down its throat. The master of ceremonies then sings:

> The children (of a socerer) are wizards.
> They forbid me to hoe with them.

Each young member of the family in turn then carries the chicken
on his shoulder, dancing with sliding steps along a circular path as
he sings. Then they kill the chicken and hurriedly prepare a soup;
each child is given a portion. After this, all the participants except
the old men go to a place outside the village where they lie on their
backs. Meanwhile, those left behind in the house sing:

> We wait for the master, until he returns.
> He returns with a goat: he returns with a cow.

Then the master of ceremonies, singing and carrying beer, the legs
of the chicken, banana stem, and a broom, leaves the house for the
spot outside the village. With the broom, he sprinkles beer over
those lying on this spot, exclaiming, "Rise whom we call to rise."
Rising up, they respond, "Thank you for coming. We would have
been lost." All then return to the hut, singing, "I come from the

abode of the dead where I looked for a cow." As a goat is placed on the unhinged door of the hut, they sing:

The bird lays eggs in a dry tree.
I myself may lay my eggs in a tree which fell down.

In other words, the dead (fallen trees) survive in their children (birds). The goat is then killed, and while they are flaying it, they sing, for the blood of the sacrificial animal will go to the spirit of the dead as an offering and a token of the covenant between the living and the dead.

Spontaneous groups such as these are motivated by community sentiments and sometimes by their reciprocal obligations within the community. Death in one family would not be the concern of only the bereaved family that has to arrange for the funeral; it would be the concern of the rest of the community as well, who will attend in sympathy and give every assistance to the family. The puberty-rite ceremony of a girl in one family will also be celebrated as a community event; other women would attend because some day it might be their turn to celebrate their daughters' puberty rites.

It is not difficult for people to come together for a particular event and to take part in the music of the occasion as required by custom. The communities in which spontaneous performing groups are formed are usually small, and individuals can be reached through established lines of communication and the network of social relations that bind them together. Messages are passed on from one person to another by word of mouth or by means of instrumental speech-surrogates such as drums, flutes, or trumpets.

The musical life of an African community is generally not left exclusively to spontaneous groups or limited to their activities. There are also organized groups, in which roles and responsibilities are distributed among members in some kind of associative relationship. Such performing groups are more or less permanent units within the social organization. When they perform in public, only those who are members can participate fully in their activities. The rest of the community are naturally attracted to them, but they come as spectators and audiences with limited opportunities for active participation.

There are two types of organized performing groups: those that exist solely for the performance of music, and voluntary associations that perform distinctive music of their own.

Musical Associations

Music societies and clubs that perform for their own enjoyment or for the entertainment of others are found in many parts of Africa. They may be invited or hired to perform on social occasions by those immediately responsible for organizing such occasions, and may perform on this basis at funerals, marriage ceremonies, or feasts. Wherever they go, they perform the music in which they specialize, regardless of the occasion.

Among the Nyasa of the Songea district of Tanzania, such associations are well organized, and music and dancing are taken seriously. According to Pamela Gulliver, every village has a dance club of some kind, either a men's club or a women's club, and musical contests are held from time to time between these clubs. Since performances are taken seriously, every club practices its art frequently, especially during the week of contest.[8]

The same sort of emphasis on music as the basis of an association appears to be true of other African countries. In Nupe country in Nigeria, such groups are identified "by the name of their leaders or by the names of the styles in which they specialise" and may enjoy the patronage of some leading personality.[9] Similarly, in Tanzania, the Nyamwezi have quite a large number of musical organizations, some of them rather similar in conception to those of the Sukuma people, such as *manyanga*, *kasomangita*, *migobo*, *buyeye*, *singoma*, *galaganza*, *masegera*, and the new popular association *hari ya mɔyɔ*.[10]

---

[8] Pamela Gulliver, "Dancing Clubs of Nyasa," *Tanganyika Notes and Records*, XLI (1955), 58–59.

[9] S. F. Nadel, *A Black Byzantium: The Kingdom of Nupe in Nigeria* (London, 1942; repr. 1969), 302.

[10] For a general discussion of categories of songs and clubs in Tanzanian

Every area in Ghana has a number of such groups, each of which specializes in the music and dance of one or two recreational musical types. In Akan communities, one may find bands specializing in *adowa, sanga, tɛtea, adenkum, kurunku, asaadua,* etc.; in Ga communities, those that specifically play *amɛdzulo, tuumatu, tsuimli,* etc.; in the Ewe area, those that especially perform *tuidzi, dedeleme, agbadza, agbekɔ, agutemi, gabu,* etc., while *tuubankpinli, dzera, bla,* and *tora* bands are found in the Dagomba area. This list can be greatly enlarged with examples from several other areas of Ghana.

The formation of musical organizations encourages creativity and innovation. Such associations may add new songs to the repertoire of an existing musical type, or as in Nupe country in Nigeria, evolve an individual style and build up a special repertoire.

Musical Specialists and Royal Musicians

The second major classification of music groups includes those attached to traditional establishments. Among these are musicians associated with occupational groups or craft guilds, such as those of Hausa country in northern Nigeria. According to David Ames, male musicians are "traditionally tied to the following craft groups whose members are patrons: (a) blacksmiths (b) butchers (c) hunters (d) musicians and praise shouters themselves and (e) farmers." [11] For each group there are prescribed sets of musical instruments. Another class of musical specialists is composed of those attached to royal courts, and of those connected to nobles or heads of leading households in stratified societies, such as praise singers, whose primary function is to maintain the oral traditions of their patrons.

Music occupies a very important place at the courts of African kings, and may form part of the integrative mechanism of traditional political systems. Some societies have mythical symbols of office which may include musical instruments. Among the Ankole

societies, see also Hans Cory, "Some East African Native Songs," *Tanganyika Notes and Records,* IV (1937), 51–64.

[11] David Ames, *A Socio-cultural View of Hausa Musical Activity* (unpublished manuscript), 10.

of Uganda, for example, this symbol is a sacred drum called *bagyendanwa*, and there is a special cult built around it.[12] The Lovedu of the Transvaal in the Republic of South Africa also have sacred drums: they are said to be four in number, and the smallest of them is mystically linked with the life of the queen and the welfare of the state.[13] Similarly, the mythical symbols of the Bambara ancestral pantheon are the *tabale* drum and the *ngoni* harp.[14]

Reigning chiefs may also be mystically related to ancestor chiefs, who continue to have a hand in the affairs of the living. In Akan society, these are represented by sacred blackened stools, each of which may have a bell attached to it for summoning the spirit of the ancestor.

Because of the religious basis of political authority, an African king may have priestly functions. He may be expected to perform or supervise the performance of certain rituals for the benefit of all. These may be private or collective public rites, and may include periodic ancestral ceremonies, rain or sowing rites, and so forth, which may be performed with music.

The integrative mechanisms of the state may also include festivals organized around major agricultural rites, officially recognized divinities, or episodes from the history and traditions of the people. Such festivals are nearly always great occasions for music making, as well as occasions for public re-enactment of the beliefs and values on which the solidarity of the state depends.

In addition to festivals, there may also be a number of ceremonies and rites designed to give opportunities for expressions of loyalty to the reigning monarch, or in the case of the monarch himself, loyalty to the state or to the ancestors. There are ceremonies and rituals concerned with the installation of kings or the assumption of other political offices, all of which are performed with music provided by musicians of the royal court.

Due regard may also be given to the king as a person, to his movements, which may be heralded by music, and to his need for relaxation and entertainment, which may also be met through

[12] K. Oberg, "The Kingdom of Ankole in Uganda," 150–57.

[13] E. J. and J. D. Krige, "The Lovedu of the Transvaal," in *African Worlds*, ed. Daryll Forde (London, 1954), 66–67.

[14] Viviana Paques, *Les Bambara* (Paris, 1954), 106–7.

music and dance. In this connection, the institution of praise singing and historical chants is a very important one, and the role of the *griot* (praise singer) is a vital one in some societies.

In the past, the kings of powerful states had an elaborate daily musical program. The kings of Dahomey, like the kings of Ashanti of old, required music at certain intervals of the day. The day began with music and ended with it; there were dinner drums at the court of the king of Ashanti, for it was customary for servants of the court to feed on his bounty, and there were talking drums, as there still are, for conveying his messages to the people.[15]

The judicial and administrative structure of the state and its organization for warfare or for the performance of other communally important tasks also had a musical counterpart. Tribunal drums were used in the Akan area of Ghana for summoning councilors to the court. In the past, a person found guilty of petty theft (such as stealing a fowl or something from the garden) was punished by being marched through the streets with the object in his hands, followed by the music of special drums. Executions of civil and war criminals were also marked by special drumming.[16]

All these called for muscial attendants at the court, men who were for the most part specialists in particular areas of musical practice. This custom has survived, and one can still find different types of royal musicians such as drummers, fiddlers, trumpeters, flutists, and so on. Some of them perform individually, while others perform in ensembles.

The freedom that such musicians have to perform on their own outside the hearing of their patrons varies from place to place. In some societies, musicians of the court can only perform their music outside the royal court with the expressed permission of their master—this is the case in the Akan area of Ghana. On the other hand, there are places where royal musicians are allowed to perform during important social events in the community and to function as entertainment groups—this is the case in Dagomba country, where royal *lunsi* (hourglass drum) players perform twice

[15] Clément da Cruz, "Les Instruments de Musique du Dahomey," *Études Dahoméennes*, XII (1954), 15–36.
[16] For the organization of Akan state drumming, see J. H. Nketia, *Drumming in Akan Communities of Ghana* (Edinburgh, 1963), 119–51.

a week in homage to their master, but are allowed to attend weddings, funerals, and other ceremonies, or to play on market days. The musicians are always busy on such occasions, for tradition allows them to accost people and drum or sing their praise names in return for gifts of money, which Dagomba custom makes obligatory.

Socio-musical Groups

In addition to purely musical groups and performers attached to establishments, there are a number of social groups—usually in the form of associations—that have their own distinctive forms of music that they perform in connection with their ceremonies and other activities. Among such groups are warrior organizations, which may be modeled on the basis of age, as in some parts of Bantu Africa, or on a territorial basis, as in the case of the Akan of Ghana. The music of such warrior organizations may reflect both their military function and the fact that in peacetime they function as associations. In Ghana, they may perform civil duties whenever required: they may be responsible for clearing paths, building bridges, organizing search parties, or dealing with other emergencies. Accordingly, their songs are varied both in style and subject matter, corresponding to the varied contexts in which they perform.

Another kind of heroic group is the hunters' association. Among the Yoruba of Nigeria, the special music of this association is *ijala*, a form of chant characterized by a large variety of texts or verses. A hunter may chant some of them while on his way to the bush. But the greatest outlet for performance is provided by the ritual and ceremonial occasion, of which there are three major types.

First, there is the onset of the Ogun festival, during which hunters, warriors, and worshipers of Ogun, the god of iron, worship together. The chants are performed during the vigil preceding the hunting expedition which is part of the festival, and also after the expedition. The hunters take turns at performing the chants to those assembled, recounting the experiences of hunters in the

Hunters' association performing the hunters' dance

bush, singing in praise of Ogun and in praise of nature or specific objects of nature such as particular animals, birds, and trees, as well as the crops that sustain hunters while out in the bush. Second, there is the occasion when hunters meet to entertain each other, or when the heads of the various hunters' associations in the whole of Yorubaland come together to consolidate their relationships and to enjoy their musical art together. Third, there are the ceremonies of the life cycle connected with the hunter and his family, when performances of *ijala* chant are sanctioned by tradition.[17]

Similar hunters' associations are found in other societies, for example, among the Ewe, Adangme, Builsa, and Akan of Ghana. To become a member of the Akan hunters' association, one must have killed a wild elephant; but to be called a master hunter, one must have killed not less than three wild elephants. There is a large

[17] A. O. Vidal, *Oriki: Praise Chants of the Yoruba*, M.A. thesis, University of California at Los Angeles (1971), 19–20.

repertoire of songs that hunters sing for their public rituals and ceremonies: songs referring to their association, experiences in the bush, the kinds of animals they hunt, and so forth.[18] When the members of such hunters' associations perform, they may be joined by their families. If an association does not have members who can play drums to accompany the songs for their dance, competent drummers may be invited to assist them.

A hunters' association is an organized group, but its members may hunt on their own or with the assistance of younger hunters-in-training. Such associations are select, and rather different from bands typical of societies like those of the Bushmen and the Pygmies, who live primarily as hunters and gatherers. But it is important to note that music plays a similarly vital role in the lives of such groups.

Cult Groups and Religious Societies

Musical activities organized around the gods that are worshiped may also form the basis of associations. These activities take various forms, and may be differentiated in intensity and duration according to the aims and purposes of worship, its public, or exclusive character. Some occasions involve no music at all, while some require music other than the special music of the gods to be used. There are occasions when both the music of the gods and other types of music may be performed, and some that make exclusive use of the music of the gods. In some societies, the same sort of music is played for all gods worshiped in a specific style, except that the songs and their texts may be varied to suit the focus of worship; there are, however, societies in which each god central to a cult has his own distinctive music.

All those who worship a particular god may form a loose association, and may be bound together simply by their common belief and dedication. Participation in the music may be defined for each worshiper by the roles that are assigned to the different groups

[18] For details of this association, see Nketia, *Drumming in Akan Communities of Ghana,* 75–89.

within the community of worshipers. In some societies, the singing is done mainly by women, while in others it is done by men or by all those present, regardless of sex. Where instruments are used, they may be played by specialists within the community of worshipers or by others recruited for the purpose.

In addition to loose cult groups formed around particular gods, secret societies or organized religious associations are found in some areas. Many of these have a fairly elaborate structure, with conditions for membership as well as procedures for admission and retention of membership, and, on occasion, external means of identification in the form of tatooing, incision, special hairdos, costumes, or special masks. Among the Sukuma of Tanzania, for example, there are a large number of such associations, each of which has its own distinctive characteristics. R. Hall gives vivid descriptions of the traits of associations in the Maswa distirct of Sukumaland in Tanzania, where one finds the *bagika, bagalu, basaji, dadono, banunguli, bagyyangi, bayeye, banyaraja, bafumu,* and *baswezi* religious societies.[19] The distinctive tatooings of the *bagika,* according to Hall, are

> a double line of incisions from right shoulder to left waist (occasionally the opposite direction also), an arrow-shaped series of incisions on the left cheek or shoulder and a zigzag line of incisions up the backs of the arms and across the shoulders.

The *bagalu* have a different set of markings, consisting of "a ring round the left eye, a double ring round the diaphram and circles on the left breast and shoulder blades." The *banunguli* have both incisions and a special hairdo. The hair is done up in tufts, and each person has "a girdle of incisions with one line above and two below on the abdomen."

Each society has its own distinctive musical type and dance, as well. Some sing and dance wearing ankle bells; others sing, drum, and dance. Although music and dance are very important activities for these societies, the basis of their association is religious or fraternal in character. They may also have practical utilitarian aims—

---

[19] R. de Z. Hall, "The Dance Societies of the Wasukuma, as Seen in the Masura District," *Tanganyika Notes and Records,* 1 (1936), 94–96.

for example, the societies that practice medicine or specialize in knowledge about snakes and their poisons and antidotes, or mutual-help societies that provide collective labor for agriculture.[20]

It will be evident from this review of the social organization of music that every member of a community could be involved in one or more of the musical events that take place in community life, for music making is related to the needs of traditional institutions and the social groups that organize their lives around them. There is music for the young, for men, for women, and for craft guilds and associations. Opportunities arise for free musical activity, for creating music outside ceremonial occasions, and for making enjoyment a basis of association.

The range of musical activities that each generation supports is not limited to items passed on to them by the previous generation. New pieces are added to the repertoire of a musical type from time to time, while others are modified or abandoned. Every so often, new musical types similarly come into vogue, while some of the existing ones lose their popularity or cease to be performed. The periodic revival of individual items or of whole categories of music takes place through the initiative of individuals, but it may also be stimulated by the recurrence of events with which such musical types are associated.

The cultivation of musical life in traditional African societies, therefore, is promoted through active participation in group life, rather than through the creation of special musical institutions. This is what forms music making in Africa into a community experience, for the continuity of musical traditions depends to some extent on both individual and collective effort. It is the creative individual who builds up the repertoire or re-creates it, but those who learn it and perform it on social occasions sustain the tradition and make it a part of the common heritage.

[20] D. W. Malcolm, *Sukumaland: An African People and Their Country* (London, 1953), 41–42.

4 / Recruitment and Training of Musicians

ALTHOUGH active participation in music making is encouraged, participation differs with respect to performing roles, and the skills and knowledge that individuals playing a given role bring to bear on a performance. Moreover, the performing roles that individuals can assume in any given situation are limited.

In vocal music, there are usually four types of performances. The first involves a soloist—solo performances in which individuals sing on their own, with or without instrumental accompaniment or even hand clapping. The solo performer may be supported by others—someone to play a bell or a drum, someone to sing answering phrases or responses at appropriate moments. Though a player of the harp lute, for example, may sing and accompany himself, he may find the need for one or more supporters. The soloist may also be accompanied by a chorus that merely chimes in here and there with a few notes at appropriate moments. In all these instances, the primary focus is on the soloist. It is he who receives public acclaim; it is his name that is associated with the performance as well as with the group as a whole. Hence, such a person would generally be regarded as a specialist and as a musician, if he satisfies other criteria to be discussed subsequently (p. 53ff.).

The second type of performance involves two people who have rehearsed together, and who share a common performance repertoire, singing in a sort of duet; but even here one might find one of them playing a lead role. The performers may sing in alternation, one echoing the other, both may sing simultaneously, or one may begin each stanza with a few notes before the second person joins in. Here the focus would be on both performers. If they perform in this manner habitually, they would invariably be regarded as musicians if they also demonstrate in their performances the attributes associated with this class of specialist (see p. 53ff.).

The third type of performance is one that emphasizes the role of a lead singer or cantor, or a number of cantors, with a supporting chorus. Here, those who habitually assume the lead role may qualify as specialists, and the chorus tends to be an undifferentiated group, in the sense that it is the group as a whole, rather than individuals, that plays specific roles. This is the case even where separate choruses are used for men and women singing in a kind of antiphony.

The fourth type of performance is one based on the interlocking principle, which establishes interdependence among the performers, making use of the *hocket* technique, whereby each singer contributes a specific note or phrase at a predetermined point. The interdependence of performers or the dependence of soloists and cantors on the support of others is formalized through an arrangement that permits soloists or cantors and their supporters or chorus to form bands or associations. The specialist takes the initiative to form the band when it consists of only a small group of performers; in other cases, someone else may take the initiative, and encourage or invite the specialist to join the band. To strengthen these relations further, patrons or elders who are not lead singers may also be invited to be members. Musical and nonmusical roles may thus be separated by assigning them to different individuals in the band or association. In whatever way a band comes to be formed, social recognition is always important for it, and opportunities for making it known and accepted are sought through public performances at ceremonies and other events. In some societies, such a band might seek recognition by finding an opportunity to perform for the chief of the area.

In instrumental music, performances may be given by individual instrumentalists or by ensembles. In the latter case, there may be an even distribution of roles—for instance, in music which employs the hocket technique. Alternatively, the organization may be based on the call-and-response form: an ensemble leader may start the music, as in the xylophone music of the Chopi of Mozambique, the music of Kontonkoli flutes, or the music of Akan flutes or trumpets. In other cases, the performer who plays the leading part does not start the music, except where he wants to give an indication of what he intends to the person who usually begins the piece; this is the arrangement in some cultures for drum music.

The leader of an instrumental ensemble would be regarded as a specialist. The members of his ensemble would also be ranked higher than the members of a chorus, and would indeed be regarded as musicians of some sort. In some musical styles, instrumental and vocal roles are combined, with the bonds that join them during performances stabilized by constituting them into a band. Attachment to a patron or some elder that they all obey helps to keep them together, and their relationships would be further strengthened through the distribution of roles and responsibilities. In such groups, musical roles are determined on the basis of executant ability, knowledge of repertoire, and skill at improvisation.

Attributes of the Musician

There are qualities or attributes that are usually expected of the musician in general, or of the specialist in particular. Examples of these from three musical cultures follow.

Among the Dagomba of Ghana, there is a class of musicians who play the hourglass-shaped drum. Bands of these drummers are led by performers whose titles differ according to the locality or the rank of the chief for whom the drummers perform.[1] The drummers are ranked in such a way that there is always a second or third person in command, and the subordinates are allowed to lead the band on certain occasions. Moreover, as the chiefs for whom drum-

[1] See Christine Oppong, "A Preliminary Account of the Role and Recruitment of Drummers in Dagbon," *Research Review*, VI/1 (1969), 38.

mers play are also ranked, a band may rise in rank as the ruler for whom it plays rises in rank in the traditional political system.

According to the Dagomba, the qualification for leadership rests on three factors. A leading drummer must know Dagomba oral literature and the traditional history of the area, in particular the chronicle of chiefs and the by-names and praise names of each of them, for a lead drummer is the person who chants these in the course of a performance.[2] Second, it is expected that he should have a sweet voice, since he has to sing; however, this is not as important as the first qualification. An experienced drummer who has knowledge of oral tradition but has a poor voice because of his age, for example, may still retain his leadership and respect among the elders of the area, even though his singing may not meet with the approval of the young people. Finally, he should have a supple wrist. That is, he must have executant ability and the skill to produce the right kinds of tones and dynamics on his drum.

When a performer has all three qualities, he is highly respected. Young people who are attracted more by the quality of the singing than by knowledge of oral literature would show their appreciation for a drummer who satisfies the ideal voice quality but lacks terseness of verbal expression or accuracy of verbal allusions.

The qualities enumerated by the Dagomba are valued in many societies, though they may be expressed in different terms. Among the Gogo of Tanzania, these qualities extend to the selective chorus. The qualifications for membership of *nindo* vocal bands include the possession of a good voice and good memory, for *nindo* songs consist of several stanzas which are taught by the composer to the group, and which have to be remembered accurately during performances. The composer usually helps the singers by *interlining* the singing (i.e., giving the singers the first few words of a stanza).

Other qualifications for membership are nonmusical. To be admitted into a *nindo* band, one must belong to the composer's particular village, or to a defined group of homesteads close to it.

---

[2] A person may have more than one name. The by-name is an alternative appelation, whereas the praise name always extols the virtue or describes a special attribute of the bearer.

There is always some kind of rivalry between village *nindo* bands for the patronage of the community as a whole, and moreso for the patronage of its leading members. But this is not the only reason for this arrangement. It is also to ensure that the composer's ideas, particularly his lyrics, are not stolen by someone from another village before the composer himself has had a chance to perform his work publicly.[3]

The third example is taken from the traditions of the Akan of Ghana. As in other societies, various categories of performers take the lead as singers, master drummers or performers on other instruments. They stand out from the chorus, which is regarded as "the children" (*gofomma*) or as followers of those who play the more distinguished roles (*gofoɔ*). A good singer is one with a good or pleasant voice (*nne a ɛyɛ dɛ*). This voice must be strong or heavy (*nne a emu yɛ duru*), not thin or small (*nne a ɛsua*). A person whose voice is thin may be quite pleasant to listen to at close quarters, but the quality of his voice does not make it easy for him to lead a chorus at a public performance, because he cannot be heard easily by members of the chorus. Another important attribute is a good ear and the ability to concentrate. A singer must not suffer from *nsoɔdɛ* (literally, "sweet ears"): that is, he must not be distracted by the parts of other performers. This applies to all musicians, singers as well as instrumentalists, for the lack of musical concentration could prevent a performer from keeping strict time, coming in at the right moment, or keeping in tune. When a performer misses the beat or his entrance, he is said to be out of step (*wafiri akyire*). However, if he uses the wrong intonation, sings wrong notes, or sings out of tune, he is said to spoil the song (*ɔsɛe dwom*).

Like the Dagomba musician, a good Akan singer must have a knowledgeable command of language. He must be able to improvise texts, to fit tunes to new words, to set tunes to words extemporaneously, and to remember texts, so that he can recall verses of songs or the leading lines. If someone who is good at this does not have the right quality of voice, he may achieve some recognition in

---

[3] See J. H. Nketia, "Multi-part Organization in the Music of the Gogo of Tanzania," *Journal of the International Folk Music Council*, XIX (1967), 79–88.

the community as a singer, and may even play the role of a lead singer who starts a song but will defer to other cantors to continue when the chorus comes in.[4]

The ability to handle texts or make appropriate references to a situation on the spur of the moment is possessed by those who have "clarity of mind" (*adwene-mu-da-hɔ*), and so do not confuse the subject or mix up words. The singer's ability to improvise reflects his alertness or presence of mind. A singer must be sensitive to or show a general awareness of current situations. Since he has to perform in public, he must not be shy when performing; indeed, some amount of histrionic temperament is said to be desirable, for a singer is involved in dramatic communication. He must act, articulate the beat in body movement, or express the depth of his musical feeling outwardly. He must be able to involve others in the music where appropriate. If he is a solo performer with no supporters or chorus of his own, he should inspire those listening to him to sing a chorus or a refrain now and then.

The Recruitment of Musicians

Since the success of a musical event depends to a large extent on good musical leadership, the recruitment of musicians is something of a prime concern to social groups, especially where performances are based on differential participation and role distribution that demand specialization. Recruitment refers to any social arrangement that ensures the availability of specialists for established roles and positions in society.

Obviously, the question of recruitment does not arise in the case of solo performers who have no attachment to a patron or to any establishment, nor does it apply to spontaneous groups who do not remain in associative relationship, for these are taken care of automatically in the institutional arrangement that governs spontaneous performances in different contexts. In all other cases, the problem lies in ensuring that there is a sufficient number of per-

[4] For a detailed discussion of this subject, see J. H. Nketia, "The Musician in Akan Society," in *The Traditional Artist in African Societies*, ed. Warren L. d'Azevedo, (Bloomington, 1972).

formers within established performing groups who satisfy the criteria of musicianship in the society and who can play the roles of specialist as required.

Where a musical band clusters around a musician who initiates it, the problem of recruitment does not arise. In other cases, however, a musician of the highest caliber will have to be encouraged to join the group through the admiration and respect that is shown for his ability, or through the size of his share of gifts that are given to the group. In some musical cultures, drummers are always given a greater share of anything that a performing group gets, since the success of a performance depends so much on them.

Similarly, socio-musical groups, such as warrior or hunters' associations, have the problem of ensuring that there are musical specialists among them to take up vital roles. Individual members who achieve reputations as lead singers or instrumentalists are encouraged to remain with the group. Where membership of a group is not voluntary, a musician of course has no choice but to provide the service that he alone can give. Cases have been noted in Ghana in which musicians who are not members of socio-musical groups play regularly for such groups by invitation.

Outside of socio-musical groups, the system of recruitment is embodied in the social organization and, in limited cases, in the social structure. In states with centralized authority, the office of the musician is generally included in the list of state functionaries. Bands of musicians responsible for particular musical types may be attached to the court either as regular servants or as servants who come to perform whenever required of them, in tribute to the ruler or the state.

The membership of a particular royal ensemble or responsibility for particular music may be organized on the basis of kinship or territory. A given household may be made responsible for maintaining a particular musical tradition, or for supplying a musician for a specific band: in Dagomba country, for instance, the son of every player of the hourglass drummer is expected to become a drummer. The daughter of a drummer is released from this obligation, but she must send a son to replace her when she has one. If she brings forth only daughters, one of them must marry a drummer, so that the descent line of drummers may continue. Recruitment is thus almost automatic, except that musical ability is a selective factor within the descent group in determining performance roles.

The transmission of roles from father to son is quite common. In some musical cultures, however, it may not necessarily be due to belief in heredity of musical talent, but simply a convenient arrangement. For example, among the Ankole of Uganda, the king's praise singers are young men recruited from the sons of the prominent men in the kingdom. Besides their musical duties, they also amuse the king by wrestling, and they follow him when he goes hunting.[5]

There is also a residence factor that affects the modes of recruitment adopted in some cultures, though this frequently correlates with the established residential patterns of descent groups. A village inhabited by a particular leading musician may take charge of specific royal musical instruments and their music. Most of the musicians of the court of the Asantehene (king of Ashanti), for example, do not live in Kumasi, the capital—they live in villages and towns around Kumasi, and the musicians who perform a particular musical type keep together in the same area as much as possible. Similarly, the principal musicians of the court of the Ankole of Uganda are recruited from the Koki district from among those who have learned to play the flute of the Baganda of Uganda.[6]

The Training of Musicians

Since musical specialists are required for group leadership and for performance in different contexts, some kind of institutional arrangement that enables musicians to acquire their technical training or that provides them with the sources of their artistic experience would seem to be of paramount importance.

The evidence available so far shows that this problem is not approached in a formal, systematic manner. Traditional instruction is not generally organized on a formal institutional basis, for it

[5] K. Oberg, "The Kingdom of Ankole in Uganda," 136.
[6] Ibid., 146.

Training the young through special performances

is believed that natural endowment and a person's ability to develop on his own are essentially what is needed. This endowment
could include innate knowledge, for according to the Akan, "One
does not teach the blacksmith's son his father's trade. If he
knows it, then it is God who taught him." Apart from the formal
training of *debteras* (professional musicians and teachers) and others
in the Ethiopian church, which has a long Christian tradition,[7] the
principle everywhere else seems to be that of learning through
social experience. Exposure to musical situations and participation
are emphasized more than formal teaching. The organization of
traditional music in social life enables the individual to acquire his
musical knowledge in slow stages and to widen his experience of

[7] See, e.g., M. Powne, *Ethiopian Music: An Introduction* (London, 1968), or
Music, Dance and Drama, Ministry of Information of Ethiopia (Adis Ababa, 1968).

the music of his culture through the social groups into which he is gradually absorbed and through the activities in which he takes part.

The African mother sings to her child and introduces him to many aspects of his music right from the cradle. She trains the child to become aware of rhythm and movement by rocking him to music, by singing to him in nonsense syllables imitative of drum rhythms. When he is old enough to sing, he sings with his mother and learns to imitate drum rhythms by rote. As soon as he can control his arm, he is allowed to tap rhythms, possibly on a toy drum. Participation in children's games and stories incorporating songs enables him to learn to sing in the style of his culture, just as he learns to speak its language.[8] His experience, even at this early age, is not confined to children's songs, for African mothers often carry their children on their backs to public ceremonies, rites, and traditional dance arenas, where they are exposed to music performed by adult groups. Sometimes the mothers even dance with their children on their backs until the children are old enough to take part in the dancing by themselves. By the time a child reaches adolescence, he may have learned to play on toy instruments by imitation, or to play minor instruments in adult ensembles. One sometimes comes across seven-year-old boys playing in drum ensembles or playing rattles for a lute player singing in a chorus, or taking quite a prominent part in a public dance. Individual instruction at this stage is unsystematic and largely unorganized. The young have to rely largely on their imitative ability, and on correction by others when this is volunteered. They must rely on their own eyes, ears, and memory, and acquire their own technique of learning.

Very often, those who attain distinction as musicians must also go through the same process. Formal systematic instruction is given only in very restricted cases demanding skills or knowledge that cannot be acquired informally, or in cases in which the specific roles played later by particular individuals make it imperative to ensure that they have acquired the necessary technique and knowl-

[8] See W. Y. Egblewogbe, *Games and Songs as an Aspect of Socialisation of Children in Eweland*, M.A. thesis, University of Ghana, 1967.

edge. Among the Akan of Ghana, for example, it is the social duty of women to mourn their kinsmen with special dirges. Many mothers, therefore, regard it as their duty to ensure that their daughters know these dirges, particularly those appropriate for mourning their parents. Accordingly, they will always find an opportunity to teach some of them to their children so that they can fulfill their social role.

Since specialization in musical instruments tends to run through families or households, children are encouraged to start learning early, especially where an instrument is believed to be difficult to master. The Chopi musicians of eastern Africa, for instance, assert that to become a really good xylophonist one must start young, preferably at the age of seven. There seems to be general agreement on this in other societies. In such instances, definite attempts at giving instruction may be made. Hugh Tracey, who has done an intensive study of Chopi musicians, tells us that among the Chopi,

> A father will take his seven or eight year old boy and sit him between his knees while he plays. The boy will hold the two beaters with his arms well-flexed and pliant while the father claps his hands over his son's and continues to play in the usual way.[9]

This is to give the child the "feel" of the instrument, so that after a few months he can play any note and learn to play simple runs and rhythms.

Similarly, the Akan child who is destined to become a player of the talking drum, for instance, is helped by the master drummer, who taps the rhythm on his shoulder blade for him to get the motor feeling involved. When he has to learn musical rhythms, he is taught appropriate sentences or nonsense syllables which convey the same sort of rhythm.[10]

Among the Baganda, it was customary for anyone who aspired to be a flutist in the royal ensemble "to be in attendance at the Palace from the age of ten to twelve years," until he had

[9] Hugh Tracey, *Chopi Musicians: Their Music, Poetry and Instruments* (London, 1948), 108.
[10] See J. H. Nketia, *Drumming in Akan Communities of Ghana*, 156.

learned to play the instrument well and had "listened to the ensemble for several years." These young musicians-in-training lived in the palace with the older musicians, who were usually their fathers or relatives. After the period of exposure and training, a young musician deemed acceptable by the older musicians was introduced to the king and sworn in as a royal musician. He then

Learning to drum

paid a fee to the head of the musical ensemble into which he had been admitted.[11]

Training by temporary affiliation seems to be an infrequent expedient in some societies. A drummer may be sent to another drummer in order to enlarge his repertoire or acquire further technique. For example, a person wishing to become a professional player of the one-string fiddle may first attach himself to a well-established musician. Musical apprenticeship, however, is not a highly developed institution. Instruction tends to be designed as part of the process by which an individual, during his entire lifetime, assimilates the traditions of his culture to the extent that he is able to express himself in terms of that tradition. Thus the learning process is not only protracted, but tends to depend rather heavily on favorable social conditions. Changes in social organization or in social life minimize the chances of learning by participation.

Moreover, the very organization of traditional music tends to impose limitations on the extent of the knowledge acquired by individuals. While women may be familiar with the music of heroic associations, for example, we would expect to find a better knowledge of this music among men. There are instances where musical knowledge belongs to esoteric groups. Hence we cannot expect single individuals, however gifted they may be, to be carriers of all the traditions of their societies.

In spite of its apparent weakness, the traditional system seemed to work well in the past, for in some cases there were religious sanctions to support it. It ensured that there were enough specialists who could perform on their own or give the required leadership. The system of recruitment tended to give some musicians group identity, particularly those related to putative ancestors. However, the development of distinctive subcultures of musicians does not seem to have been encouraged, although there is now evidence of the emergence of this in some societies such as those of the Tiv and the Hausa of Nigeria.

Traditional musicians have continued to play a very important role in community life and to receive the recognition due to them as

---

[11] Lois Anderson, *The Miko Modal System in Baganda Xylophone Music*, Ph.D. dissertation, University of California at Los Angeles, 1968.

specialists. They are often rewarded for their services in the form of gifts or fees, and privileges may also be accorded them by members of their performing groups, or in some cases by the society as a whole. Attitudes to musicians, however, tend to be ambivalent when their social behavior is also taken into account. This is particularly true of itinerant musicians, who tend to be conspicuous because of the instruments they carry about with them. They are praised for their music, but not always admired for their conduct. In some societies they are believed to be somewhat bad-tempered, demanding, and even rude when convenient, as well as lazy, because they spend all their time making music.

Players of solo instruments are sometimes associated with excesses, particularly in regard to their drinking habits. This is the case with players of some chordophones, and to some extent those master drummers who do not have any reason to be abstemious. There is not much evidence that musicians are conscious of this social image of themselves, or that they try to live up to it; but they are conscious of their roles and duties and of the recognition that is due to them. That is why an Akan drummer may remind his audience that, in the language of proverbs,

> Ever since the Creator created the world,
> Ever since the manifold Creator created the world,
> The drummer is treated gently and kindly.
> A person becomes a drummer that he may get something
>   to eat.
> If you wish to catch the monkey,
> Give it ripe plantain.

SECTION TWO / *Musical Instruments*

5 / Instrumental Resources

THE instrumental resources at the disposal of performers naturally tend to be limited to those in which their respective communities specialize. They may be instruments believed to be of local origin, or instruments which have become integrated into the musical life of their communities from other areas. They may show local peculiarities in design and construction as well as in tuning, for every society maintains its own norms or accepts creative innovations in its musical practice or instumental types, without reference to other societies with whom they have minimal cause for musical contact. Taken together, however, similarities in the basic features of instruments, even from widely separated areas, are striking.

It must also be noted that, while the aggregate of instrumental resources used throughout Africa is quite large, the assortment used by individual societies is limited to a small selection from the four main instrumental classes to be discussed subsequently. This limitation may be related to environmental factors, to the kind of occupation in which a society engages, or to historical factors. There are nomadic societies, for example, that have no drums; many of them are content to use the sticks and other implements they carry with them for musical purposes. Their rhythmic interests are displayed in hand clapping, complex body movements, rhythmic stamping, and even the use of vocal grunts. Striking differences are sometimes evident in the musical resources of savannah dwellers and those who live in the forest, particularly in the types and range of membranophones that are developed, the types of skins that are used for covering resonators, and so on.

Environmental limitations are, of course, not always insurmountable. They may be overcome through trade and other activities that bring members of different musical cultures into contact with one another. Accordingly, some instruments tend to be concentrated in areas of intensive cultural interaction, in which societies living in close proximity borrow from each other.

It will be evident from the foregoing observations that the study of musical instruments may be approached from different angles. It may be viewed historically, in terms of origin and development, or culturally, in terms of social uses, functions, and the beliefs and values associated with them. Musical instruments may also be studied as material objects in terms of their technology, with respect to their design and craftsmanship, materials and construction, and musical function.

As the literature on African music abounds in detailed studies of the musical instruments of particular regions and societies, we shall confine ourselves in the succeeding chapters to a brief inventory of African musical instruments, limiting our observations primarily to the uses to which instruments are put and to the basis of their selection.

6 / *Idiophones*

OF the variety of instruments found in Africa, the idiophones are the most common, for they include the simplest as well as the most easily improvised sound producing objects. An idiophone (literally, "self sounding") may be broadly defined as any instrument upon which a sound may be produced without the addition of a stretched membrane or a vibrating string or reed. Societies that have no drums or other instruments can resort to these idiophones for accompanying their songs, while those that have other instruments may reinforce the rhythmic foundation of their music with them.

Of course, their use is not confined to purely musical functions. Some are used where appropriate as signals for attracting attention, assembling people, or creating an atmosphere (especially during religious rites and ceremonies). They may also be used for transmitting verbal messages or for reinforcing verbal communication, for marking the movements of special personalities such as priests and persons undergoing sacred initiations, or for emphasizing the movements of a dancer or a character in traditional drama. In some societies, appropriate idiophones are used for scaring birds away from newly ploughed fields, or for marking the movements of cattle and other animals (or even domestic birds) that need to be watched or identified.

Except where idiophones are used as aids to the farmer or the pet owner, or where they are treated purely as symbolic objects rather than as sound producers, the instruments may function simultaneously in a musical context for communication and dramatic emphasis.

From the musical point of view, two major categories of idiophones need to be distinguished: those used mainly as rhythm instruments, and those played independently as melodic instruments.

Shaken Idiophones

Of the idiophones used principally as rhythm instruments, the most common and widely used appear to be shaken idiophones, or rattles. Functionally, they can be subdivided into two major groups: primary rattles, which are held in the hand and played, and secondary rattles, which are worn on the body of performers and activated by their movements, or attached to other instruments as "modifiers." A secondary rattle in the form of jingling metals may be tied to the wrists of a xylophone player or an hourglass drummer. Similarly, a drum may have jingling discs fastened to the rim or placed on the head like a snare (see illustration on p. 88), as a plucked lute may have such a rattling device attached to the tip of its neck.

Primary rattles include the gourd variety, which may appear as container rattles or as rattles surrounded by nets of cowries, sea shells, pieces of bone, bamboo shoot, metal, or beads. A gourd rattle may be spherical, either without a handle or with the neck of the gourd or calabash serving as the handle. They come in different sizes; among the largest are the *sekere* rattles of the Yoruba of Nigeria and the Nago of Dahomey.

Among the other varieties of container rattles are wicker rattles, reed-box rattles (found mainly in eastern Africa), and seed-shell rattles. One or more of the latter may be strung together by a rope or held together by means of a stick serving as a handle. There are also *baobab*-seed rattles, various metal jingles, and bowl rattles, as well as stick or rod rattles, made by threading a number of calabash discs on a stick.

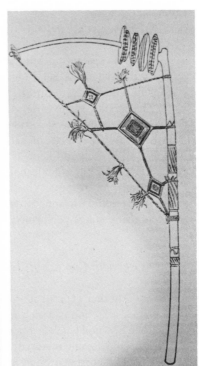

Gourd rattle enmeshed in a net of beads

ABOVE RIGHT: sistrum from
Kissi country in Guinea
BELOW RIGHT : Ethiopian sistrum

The sistrum, a kind of rattle with metal discs suspended on fixed rods, has a very important place in Ethiopian church worship, and is also found in various forms in parts of west Africa.[1] The west-African variety may have a shape and arrangement of metal discs identical to that of the Ethiopian Church, or it may be made out of pieces of calabash strung on the thinner part of a forked branch and kept in position by a cord tied from the end of this stick to the stem (see illustration on p. 71). In Kissi country in Guinea, for example, this kind of sistrum is decorated and used in connection with some rituals and ceremonies of the life cycle to accompany songs performed for dances and processions.[2]

Struck and Concussion Idiophones

Another type of idiophone commonly found in Africa is the struck idiophone, which may take the form of a resonant slab of stone or wood (such as the *merewa* of Ethiopia [3]) struck by a smaller piece of the same material, of multiple rock gongs such as those observed in northern Nigeria,[4] or of rock gongs and stone clappers, such as those played in the religious service of some Yoruba cults.[5] This group also includes two round sticks of the same size which are struck together, two flat sticks struck together as clappers, or a percussion beam around which a number of people squat and strike rhythmically with sticks. Still other varieties consist of iron or wooden bells with clappers, as well as clapperless iron bells struck with sticks, rods, or small animal horns. There are single clapperless bells—usually shaped like a cone or a boat—and double bells (see illustration on p. 113). The latter appears in the form of

---

[1] See Ashenafi Kebede, "La musique sacrée de l'Eglise Orthodoxe de l'Ethiopie," in *Ethiopie: Musique de l'Eglise Copte* (Berlin, 1969), 7, and Michael Powne, *Ethiopian Music: An Introduction.*

[2] See André Schaeffner, *Les Kissi: Une Société Noire et Ses Instruments de Musique* (Paris, 1951), 13–19.

[3] Ministry of Information of Ethiopia, *Music, Dance and Drama in Ethiopia,* 16.

[4] Bernard Fagg, "The Discovery of Multiple Rock Gongs in Nigeria," *African Music,* I/3 (1956), 6–9.

[5] Anthony King, "A Report on the Use of Stone Clappers for the Accompaniment of Sacred Songs," *African Music,* II/4 (1961), 64–71.

two metal cones mounted on a single frame, or two bells held together by an arch.

Single and double clapperless bells vary in size. Very large ones are used in some ritual and court music: three are played by the ritual attendants (*nsumankwaafoɔ*) of the court of the Asantehene of Ghana, and four are played in an ensemble with a drum by the Bumum of the Cameroons.[6]

Sometimes the blades of a hoe, animal horns, or tortoise shells are used instead of bells. Various types of bell-like iron castanets played in west Africa also belong to this group. They consist of two pieces: a metal ring worn on the thumb or held in the same hand as a small round bell about the size of a lemon, or a somewhat long conical bell constructed in such a way that it can be worn on the middle finger.

Another important instrument in the subgroup of struck idiophones is the wooden slit drum. It is made out of a hollowed log of wood, a section of which is slit open to provide it with a pair of "lips" that can be struck with beaters. This pair of "lips" may be

Playing a finger bell, or a bell resembling a castanet

<hr>

[6] Francis Bebey, *Musique de l'Afrique* (Paris, 1969), 126.

constructed so as to yield two or sometimes four contrasting tones. These instruments can also be made out of bamboo, and may appear in different sizes. They are found in west Africa—Guinea, Sierra Leone, Liberia, eastern Nigeria, and the Cameroons—as well as in central Africa. They are used both as musical instruments and as speech surrogates; in central Africa, for example, they function as the principal talking drums of the Lokele and other societies.[7]

Other types of struck idiophones include gourd percussion—an upturned calabash usually struck with thin sticks, or in some cases with a wire broom.[8] In Manding country (in the savannah belt of west Africa), this calabash may also be upturned on a cushion.[9] A sound closer to that of a skin drum is produced by placing such a calabash in a bowl of water. Another functional substitute for the skin drum is found among the Ijaw of Nigeria, and consists of clay pots of different sizes filled with water and struck at the mouth with special fan-like beaters.

A few concussion idiophones are also found. They include iron cymbals noted in Ghana at the court of Ashanti kings, and concussion idiophones made by connecting two small gourds or

Scraped idiophone, consisting of a notched stick passed through a scraper; beside it, a fruit shell used for varying the tone

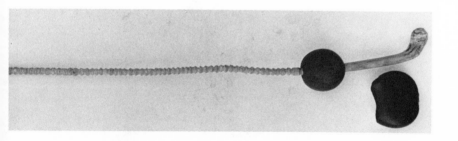

[7] J. F. Carrington, *Talking Drums of Africa* (London, 1949).
[8] Robert and Pat Rizzentheler, *Music of the Cameroons*, album notes (Ethnic Folkways, FE 4372).
[9] Guy Atkins, ed., *Manding: Focus on an African Civilization* (London, 1972).

fruit shells with strings. The latter may also contain pebbles or seeds, and so function as concussion rattles.

Scraped and Friction Idiophones

Other idiophones played in African societies include the rasp, a piece of notched bamboo or palm stem scraped with another stick, or, as noted in Cameroons, with a bracelet of brass, or a notched stick scraped by being passed through a fruit shell. In this case the tone may be varied by pressing and releasing a flat piece of hollow fruit shell at one end of the rasp.

Instrumental sounds are also obtained by scraping a bottle with the lid of a tin, by rubbing a calabash or gourd against a board, or by rubbing a board on which some charcoal has been sprinkled with friction sticks.

Stamped Idiophones

Another category of idiophones found at musical performances is the stamped idiophone. There are two main types: stamping sticks and stamping tubes. Stamping sticks are used for hitting the ground, usually in vertical motion, to produce a sound

Stamped idiophone: *adenkum*

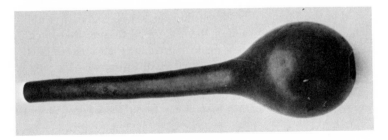

for accompanying singing—in some societies, old pestles are used as stamping sticks. One of the two forms of stamping tubes consists of a piece of bamboo tube cut so that only one end of it is open. To produce a sound, the closed end is hit at an inclined position against hard ground, or preferably against a slab of stone. Among the Ga of Ghana, this bamboo stamping tube is used for accompanying female choruses, and a suitable slab of stone is always carried to the performance arena. About three bamboo tubes tuned to different pitches are played together, each one playing a different rhythmic pattern.

The second type of stamping tube is made out of an elongated gourd, or a gourd with a long narrow neck. The tip of the gourd is sliced off to make it open-ended, and the opening is cupped by the free hand. A small hole is also cut at the base of the gourd, enabling the performer to get a variety of tones from the instrument. One tone is produced by striking the bottom of the gourd against the bare thigh; another is produced when it is lifted from the thigh and hit with the cupped hand; and a third, when the bulbous end is hit against the arm or elbow by a drop action of the wrist, or is slapped with the fingers. A rhythmic pattern is built out of all these sounds for accompanying singing.

Stamped idiophones made out of gourds are played in Ghana by Ashanti women, who call such an instrument *adenkum*, [10] and in Nigeria by Hausa women, who call them *shantu*. [11] In details of form and playing techniques, however, the two are not identical.

Tuned Idiophones

The idiophones considered thus far are played as rhythm instruments. Although each of them is tuned to a desired pitch or tone complex, no attempt is made to graduate their tones or pitches in such a way that they can be used as substitutes for the singing

[10] For a detailed study of this instrument and its music see B. A. Aning, *Adenkum: A Study of Akan Female Bands*, Thesis for the University of Ghana Diploma in African Music, 1964.

[11] See Mercedes Mackay, "The Shantu Music of the Harems of Nigeria," *African Music*, I/2 (1955), 56–57.

voice. Instruments in the same family that can be used for playing melodies are tuned idiophones, of which there are two types: the *mbira* or *sansa* (hand piano) and the xylophone.

Varieties of these are used for simulating drumming as well as for playing melodies, particularly the large box *sansa* with three to five keys, used in west Africa to accompany singing. In addition to plucking the keys with one hand, the performer may hit the box itself with the free hand, in order to produce an effect similar to that of an ensemble of two or three drummers playing in a polyrhythmic style. Similarly, the edge of a xylophone key may be struck with a hard stick (often the hard end of a xylophone beater), in order to produce a penetrating percussive sound which serves as a rhythmic accompaniment to the melody played on the xylophone with the soft end of the beater. Both of these usages highlight the essential character of these two instruments: while they are basically tuned percussion, the intensity of their sounds is exploited in the rhythmic organization of their music.

Mbira (*Sansa*, hand piano)

The melodic type of *mbira* consists of a graduated series of wooden or metal lamellae (strips) arranged on a flat sounding board and mounted on a resonator such as a box, a gourd, or even a tin. The wooden lamellae may be made out of strips of the bark of rafia palm or rattan cane, while the metal keys may be made out of iron or, in somewhat rare cases, brass.[12] Rattling pieces of metal, a chain, or a number of snail shells may be attached to the sounding board or to the resonator to increase the ratio of noise to pitch; a similar effect is produced by winding little strips of light metal loosely around the base of each key.

An *mbira* may have from one to three manuals, and a single-manual *mbira* may have between five and twenty keys, with manuals of eight to twelve keys most common. Large *mbiras* of thirty-four to forty-five keys occur among the Gogo of Tanzania, though

---

[12] See Hugh Tracey, "The Mbira Class of Instruments in Rhodesia," *African Music*, IV/3 (1969), 78–95.

Mbira (sansa) with
box resonator

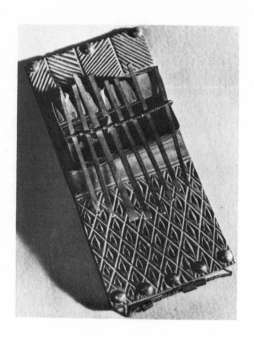

some of the keys, particularly those of the middle row, appear to be assembled for the purpose of increasing the volume of sound through sympathetic vibration. The most complex or sophisticated *mbira* types are found in Rhodesia and adjacent territories, where *mbiras* of more than one manual are played. The two-manual *mbira* of the Shona-Karanga (the *njari*), for example, has twenty-three to twenty-nine keys, while that of the Nyanja has twenty-seven keys.[13]

The tuning of *mbiras* is by no means uniform. Each society tunes its instruments according to the scales in common use by its musicians. Measurements taken by Hugh Tracey of a wide variety of tunings show that the patterns of tuning are generally pentatonic (five-tone), hexatonic (six-tone) or heptatonic (seven-tone);[14] the actual intervals these patterns represent show a much more complex picture than this. Moreover, in the actual tuning of these instruments, it is not always the fundamental pitch that is consid-

[13] Ibid., 88–89.
[14] Hugh Tracey, "Towards an Assessment of African Scales," *African Music*, II/1 (1958), 15–20.

ered, but sometimes the overtones as well—in other words, the entire tone complex is relevant. This has a bearing on the concept of chords and chordal sequences used in *mbira* music, since two notes played together represent not just two pitches, but a harmonic complex.[15]

The arrangement of the keys follows the two sections of the fingerboard, the dividing line being the lowest-pitched note. The section on the left is played with the left hand, by the thumb alone or with the forefinger, while the section on the right is played with the right hand, by the thumb alone or with the forefinger. The arrangement in order of pitch of the sequence of keys in each section is by no means uniform throughout Africa. In some cases, adjacent keys do not represent adjacent notes of the scale: one step may be missing. In a heptatonic tuning, for example, each row would be in sequence of ascending thirds, with the highest-pitched keys in the outer extreme of the fingerboard. Thus if the lowest key in the middle is, for example, C, the row to the left of it may be arranged in a rising sequence of thirds as E–G–B–D', while those to the right of it are arranged as D–F–A–C'–E'.

In the more complex *mbiras* of Rhodesia and adjacent territories, on the other hand, the pattern of the layout is guided by the hierarchic function of pitches in the melodic and harmonic configurations that are built up in the music. Notes which function principally as bass notes are distinguished from the melody notes of the middle range and the high-pitched notes that duplicate some of these; thus, in the layout of some of these *mbiras*, duplicated notes may lie on either side of the fingerboard. Furthermore, the octaves of notes in the lower manual may be arranged directly above the notes; and in each section of the layout, adjacent keys generally represent adjacent notes of the scale.[16] All these indicate the degree

[15] See Robert A. Kauffman, *Multi-Part Relationships in the Shona Music of Rhodesia*, Ph.D. dissertation, University of California at Los Angeles, 1970, 84.

[16] For a detailed description of *mbira* instruments and music, see the following by Andrew Tracey: "Mbira Music of Jege A. Tapera," *African Music*, II/4 (1961), 44–63; "The Tuning of Mbira Reeds," *African Music*, IV/3 (1969), 96–100; "The Matepe Mbira Music of Rhodesia," *African Music*, IV/4 (1970), 37–61; and "Three Tunes on the Mbira Dza Vadzimu," *African Music*, III/2 (1963), 23–26. See also Hugh Tracey, "The Mbira Class of Instruments in Rhodesia," *African Music*, IV/3 (1969), 78–95.

A frame xylophone of fourteen keys; note the graduated gourd resonators

of musicianship that the mastery of *mbira* music demands of the performer. A simple-looking *mbira* may be quite a sophisticated instrument in terms of its technical demands.

The *mbira* is played for personal enjoyment or for social occasions of a recreational nature; but there are types such as the *mbira dza Vadzimu* that are played on other occasions, such as ancestral rituals.

Xylophones

Another important tuned idiophone played in many African societies is the xylophone, which appears in three forms. In the first type, the gradated series of wooden slabs or keys are mounted over a resonance chamber such as a pit, a box or trough, or a clay pot. Pit xylophones are found in a few places in west Africa (Guinea, Nigeria, and Chad), in the Central African Republic (among the Azande and the Kala), and in Kenya (among the Kusu). Box xylophones are played by the Zaramo of Tanzania, while xylophone keys tied over pots are found in Iboland in Nigeria.

In the second type of xylophone, the keys are laid over two pieces of banana stems and are kept in position by sticks affixed to the stem between the keys. This is common in west Africa (for example, in Kissi country in Guinea and in the Ivory Coast), as well as in central and eastern Africa (e.g., Zaire, Uganda, Tanzania, and Mozambique).

The third type has keys mounted over a wooden frame, below which a number of gourd resonators are suspended, gradated in size in relation to the pitches of the wooden slabs. It has a wide distribution in west Africa, as well as in central and eastern Africa—from Zaire to Mozambique, and further south to Vendaland.

The number of slabs used for constructing African xylophones varies. Some xylophones have a narrow compass of one to four keys; these may be found among the Ibo of Nigeria, the Bariba of Dahomey, the Kabere of Togo, the Baule of Ivory Coast, and the Nsenga and Valley Tonga of Zambia. Xylophones with ten to twenty-two keys have a wider distribution, being played by the Ganda of Uganda (the twenty-two-key *akadinda*), the Chokwe of Angola (seventeen keys), the Pende of Zaire (seventeen keys), the Chopi of Mozambique (ten, twelve, sixteen, and nineteen keys), the Venda of South Africa (twenty keys), the Lobi-Dagarti and Sisala of Ghana (fourteen, seventeen, and twenty-two keys), the Bambara of Mali (sixteen keys), and the Sara of Chad (fourteen keys), to name a few.

Xylophones are usually tuned progressively from low notes to high (or from large slabs to small), but this is by no means invariable. Among some societies of the Cameroons, they may also be tuned in octave pairs; that is, a key and the next higher octave are placed together, with a little gap left between this pair and the next.

In some societies, such as those of northwestern Ghana, small and large xylophones are sometimes kept separate, because their keys begin on different pitches and are therefore not played together. In other societies, this differentiation is conceived of in relation to musical roles in ensembles. Among the Chopi, for example, there are treble xylophones with sixteen keys, alto xylophones with nineteen keys (that is, with three additional lower keys), tenor xylophones of twelve keys (with two keys lower than the alto xylophone), bass xylophones with ten keys (two of which are lower in pitch than those of the tenor xylophone), and a contrabass xylophone with four keys (beginning two steps below the bass).[17]

A similar distribution exists in other xylophone cultures having three or four types of instruments, except that the compass of those instruments that play accompanying notes or ostinati may be reduced to the basic notes that they are generally required to play. This scheme is also utilized where xylophones of the narrow compass of two or three keys are played in ensembles: the instruments are tuned in such a way that when they are played together, they can share the notes of the melody, as well as those of the accompanying figures.

As with the *mbira* and indeed other melodic instruments, the tuning system of xylophones may be pentatonic, hexatonic, or heptatonic. Both equidistant and nonequidistant tunings are utilized,

---

[17] See Hugh Tracey, *Chopi Musicians*, 120.

although the trend towards a kind of equidistant tuning is apparently widespread.[18] Equidistance in this context does not mean that the intervals are absolutely equal; disparities will be found between them, partly because the intervals are not calibrated, and partly because what is aimed at is generally gross tuning within the pattern, rather than absolute pitches. An equidistant tuning, in the African context, is a system of tuning which is based not on a concept of small and large intervals, but on the recognition of steps that resemble one another (cf. p. 117). When a key does not conform to this step system but is retained on the instrument as something tolerable, it is referred to as a "bad" key.

Among the Lobi of Ghana, there is another kind of "bad" key. It occurs in one particular xylophone tuned to a tetratonic scale, and is purposely placed after each set of four keys, counting from the bottom. If the "bad" keys are played, they change the scale from a tetratonic to a pentatonic one; but because they are not supposed to be played, they are described as keys to be avoided. "Bad" keys are built into the design merely to give the standard number of keys and facilitate the motor movement that controls the formation of melodic phrases.

The use of some kind of equidistant tuning facilitates transposition. For example, among the xylophone cultures of Ghana, the normal starting position of a melody may be shifted up or down to agree with the voices of the singers, or to counteract the effect of changes in temperature on the instrument. Such a standardized tuning system also facilitates the use of polyphony, since a number of melodic fragments can be played against each other.

In addition to differences in tuning, differences in quality between various types of African xylophones are also noticeable. Much depends on the resonance of the wood, as well as the choice of resonators: log or leg xylophones, for instance, do not sound the same as frame xylophones. Likewise, in the case of frame xylophones, one would notice appreciable differences in quality between xylophones whose gourd resonators have buzzers (spider's-nest membranes, which produce a buzzing sound) attached to them and those which do not have this device.

[18] See A. M. Jones, *Africa and Indonesia*.

Xylphones may be played as solo instruments or in small ensembles of two, three, or four instruments. Large ensembles ranging from ten or fifteen to as many as thirty xylophones are found in eastern Africa, particularly among the Chopi, who are well known for their sophisticated xylophone music. In some traditions, such as those of Uganda, a number of performers may play a single instrument. Three players play the *amadinda*, while as many as six performers play the *akadinda*. In the *amadinda* styles, two players sit abreast, while one sits opposite them; in the *akadinda* type, the players sit three abreast, opposite three others. Each player has his own playing area (that is, a set of keys that only he plays), as well as his own part.

Xylophones are played by themselves or in combination with other instruments. They may be accompanied by a rhythm section consisting of drums and rattles, or drums, bells, and castanets or percussion sticks, or they may be combined with other melodic instruments. Available recordings demonstrate combinations of xylophone and *mbira*, as well as xylophones and harp lutes; combinations of xylophone and voice, either solo or chorus, are also common.

In areas where they are the principal instruments, xylophones may be played in a variety of ritual contexts, as well as for recreation. In some societies such as those of northwestern Ghana, they may also be used for making special announcements, especially for funerals, by playing any of a number of tunes set aside for this purpose. The melody would indicate whether a man, a woman, an old person, or a child has died.

7 / Membranophones

In many African societies, the emphasis on percussive instruments finds it highest expression in the use of membranophones (drums with parchment heads). These instruments range from simple makeshift types played by women in ritual contexts, like skin aprons stretched over pots or oxhide stretched on poles, to specially constructed instruments with elaborate decorations, treated as objects of art.[1]

Drums are usually carved out of solid logs of wood; they may also be made out of strips of wood bound together by iron hoops. Earthernware vessels are used as drum shells as well, while potsherd is used as a hoop for making round frame drums. Another material used for making membranophones is the large gourd or calabash; this is very common in the savannah belt of west Africa. In modern times, various hollow vessels have been used in a few isolated cases as substitutes. The use of tins, light oil drums, and other such materials has been noted in Ghana and Kenya.[2] Toy drums for little children, which used to be made out of hard fruit

---

[1] Makeshift drums are found in a few places in eastern and southern Africa, specifically in Ankole, Kiga, Usindja, and Iraku country in Uganda, and among the Xhosa of South Africa: see K. P. Wachsmann, "The Sound Instruments," in *Tribal Crafts of Uganda*, ed. Margaret Trowell and K. P. Wachsmann (London, 1958), II, 311–422.

[2] Graham Hyslop, *Musical Instruments of Kenya*, unpublished manuscript.

shells or other natural hollow vessels, may now be made out of discarded tins.

Drums appear in a wide variety of shapes. They may be conical, cylindrical, or semicylindrical, with a bulge in the middle or a bowl-shaped top, cup-shaped, bottle-shaped, in the form of a goblet or vase, or in the shape or an hourglass; the frames may be round or square. All these are made in different sizes. There are drums that are small or light enough to be held in one hand and played with the other, or held under the armpit when played, sling drums, and heavy drums of various types, which are normally placed on the ground when played. Some cylindrical or semicylindrical drums measure about five or six feet high and twenty-four inches across, and large drums may be four feet tall with a diameter of thirty inches.

Some of these drums are single-headed, open at one end and closed at the other end by means of a board or a nonsonorous skin; others are double-headed drums, or drums with sonorous skins at both ends. The manner in which the drum head is fixed varies. It may be glued down to the shell, nailed down by thorns or nails, or suspended by pegs that can be pushed in or out to regulate its tension. The head may also be laced down by thongs to a tension ring at the bottom, or to another skin at the other end; the lacing may be Y-shaped, W-shaped, or occasionally X-shaped.

Although a wide variety of drums exists in Africa, each society usually specializes in a small number of drum types. Nevertheless, the provenance of some of these drums tends to be less localized. For example, hourglass-shaped drums are found in both eastern and western Africa. Moreover, many examples of those found in eastern Africa are single-headed; when two heads are used, they are not treated as they are in west Africa, as tension drums.[3]

The distribution of drums of particular design and construction tends to be restricted to limited geographical areas. The Ugan-

---

[3] Tension drums are double-headed drums whose heads are held together by a number of thongs running from one head to the other, but which are designed in such a way that they can be used to regulate the tension of the heads through the application of pressure from the hand or the arms when placed under the armpit.

Hourglass drummers

dan drum, for example, is peculiar to eastern Africa. Outside of
Uganda, versions of it are found in Ethiopia, as well as in Kenya
and Burundi. Similarly, other varieties of small hand drums are
found in different parts of eastern Africa. In Ethiopia, the *atamo* is
held in the hand and played with the fingers or palm of the free
hand, or held under the armpit and played with both hands. In
Uganda, a version of this drum (called *ntimbo*) is similarly held
under the arm "on leather belts slung over the left shoulder and
beaten with both hands." [4] Among the Nyisansu of Tanzania, it is
held in one hand and beaten with the free hand or with a leather
thong. Likewise, drums that look very much alike are played in
the savannah belt of west Africa. They include long, narrow
drums and shorter, cup-shaped drums, both played by hand, a
number of double-headed drums, and single-headed gourd drums.

An important consideration in the design and construction of
drums is the question of tone quality and pitch. The choice of different shapes and sizes of drums, as well as the choice of drum
heads and methods of holding the drum head, are generally made

[4] K. P. Wachsmann, "The Sound Instruments," 367.

Tanzanian hand drum

Ugandan drum

Atumpan drums, with a jingling metal affixed
to the lower-pitched drum

with this in mind. Sometimes additional devices are used to get specific qualities of sound: for example, seeds or beads may be deposited in the shell of a closed drum, as in the Ethiopian *atamo* hand drum or the Hausa hourglass drum used by the praise singer. Rattling metals or jingles may be attached to the rim of a drum, as is the practice in Senegal, Guinea, and Mali; or, instead of a rattling metal, little bells may be used, as in the Yoruba *iya ilu* drum. A jingle may also be suspended across the drum head, as in the case of the *akasaa* placed on the male (in this case, low-pitched) *atumpan* drum used by the Akan of Ghana.

The playing techniques that are applied to particular drums may also be chosen with the sonorities of the drum in mind. Some drums are played with sticks—straight and round sticks with or without a knob at the end, or curved or slightly bent sticks—with the weight of the stick depending entirely on the drum. Other drums are played by hand, or stick and hand combined. The use of the cupped hand, the palm, palm and fingers, or the base of the palm in different positions on the drum affect tone quality and pitch; this is applicable only to drums capable of distinctive variations in sonority.

Although most drums are played by percussive means, there are special drums that are played by friction. Among the Akan of Ghana, for example, the *etwie* friction drum is played by rubbing the drum head (on which powder has been sprinkled) with a stick. In eastern and central Africa, a cord or stick which runs through the center of a friction drum is rubbed with wet hands to activate the membrane.

Drums may be played singly, in pairs, or in larger ensembles. In the latter case, the drums grouped together are usually graded in tone and pitch, so that each one can be heard in specific positions in which tone or pitch contrasts are desired. In some cultures in eastern Africa, these contrasts are provided by individual players playing on a set of tuned drums in a kind of hocket arrangement. The most outstanding of these are the set of fifteen *entenga* drums of the Kabaka (king) of Uganda. The drums are tuned to definite pitches, and are used for playing tunes similar in form and structure to those played by xylophones. Twelve of the drums comprise the main melody section and are played by four drummers, each of whom

Set of tuned drums (drum chime) from Digo country in Kenya

has a playing area of five drums. The three drums of the rhythm section are played by two people: one plays only one drum, while the other plays the remaining two—a small and a big drum.[5]

Smaller sets of tuned drums have also been observed in Uganda: the *namaddu* drum chime (set of tuned drums) of the Gwere consisting of five drums, and the seven-drum chime of the Lango. Similarly tuned drums are found in Digo country in Kenya and in Zaramo country in Tanzania.[6]

In addition to their musical uses, the sounds of membranophones may function as speech surrogates or as signals (call signals, warning signals, etc.).[7] Other uses of drums, especially for nonverbal communication, occur in a few societies, which make special drums for symbolic and representational purposes. For example,

[5] K. P. Wachsmann, "Some Speculations Concerning a Drum Chime in Baganda," *Man*, I (1965), 1–8.

[6] Graham Hyslop, "More Kenya Musical Instruments," *African Music*, II/2 (1959), 27.

[7] J. H. Nketia, "Surrogate Languages of Africa," *Current Trends in Linguistics*, VII (1971), 699–732.

the *etwie* friction drum of the Akan is supposed to imitate the snarl of the leopard; therefore, it is played to extol the might and majesty of the king. Another royal drum called *aburukuwa* is supposed to imitate the cry of a bird of similar name. Other examples of symbolic or representational use of membranophones occur among the Lovedu, the Ankole, and the Bambara.[8]

• [8] See E. J. and J. D. Krige, "The Lovedu of the Transvaal," 66–67; K. Oberg, "The Kingdom of Ankole in Uganda," 150–57; and Viviana Paques, *Les Bambara*, 106–7.

8 / *Aerophones*

In addition to idiophones and membranophones, many African societies make use of a limited number of aerophones (wind instruments). These fall into three broad groups.

The Flute

The first group includes instruments of the flute family, made from materials with a natural bore, such as bamboo, the husk of cane, the stalks of millet, or the tip of a horn or gourd; alternatively, they may be carved out of wood. Occasionally, one comes across the use of metal tubing as a substitute for the bamboo flute.[1] There are also clay flutes and ocarinas (round or oval-shaped instruments with finger holes and a mouth hole) made out of the shells of fruit.

Flutes may be open-ended or stopped, and may be designed for playing in vertical or transverse position. The embouchure (mouthpiece) of vertical or end-blown flutes may be notched or round, while the number of finger holes provided for each type of

---

[1] The use of metal pipes has been observed in northern Ghana among the Dagomba, and in Tanzania among the Zaramo. It appears that the *embilta* of Ethiopia, which is normally made of bamboo, may also be made out of metal pipe. See J. Courlander, *Folk Music of Ethiopia*, album notes (Ethnic Folkways, FE 4405).

End-blown notched flute

flute depends on the way the individual instrument is used. Flutes
of wide compass usually have four to six finger holes, and flutes
with fewer holes can have their ranges extended by the technique
of overblowing. There are also flutes of narrow compass, with a
range of two or three tones, as well as others that play only one
note. These are often made in sets of different pitches, so that a
number of them can be combined to play melodies of a wider
compass through the use of the hocket technique. Panpipes (sets of
single-tone flutes bound together and played by a single performer)
are not as common as solo flutes or sets of flutes played hocket-
fashion by a number of performers. However, panpipes do occur
among a few societies in widely separated areas on the continent,

93

such as among the Soga of Uganda, the Yombe of Zaire, and the Pedi of South Africa; a few examples also occur in west Africa.

Flutes may be used as solo instruments for playing fixed tunes or improvised pieces, for conveying signals, or for superimposing sounds on the music of an ensemble in order to create a definite mood or atmosphere. They may also be conceived of as an integral part of the melody section of an ensemble. Flutes are played in duets as well (as one finds, for example, among the Baule of Ivory Coast), or in ensembles of three or more instruments. In the latter case, the extent of the individual instruments' ranges is sometimes relative to their musical roles: the leading instrument may cover the entire compass, while the others are limited to a few notes that they play in response. Flutes are combined in ensemble with drums, with voices, or with both, and with lyre, drums, and rattles.

Reed Pipes

The second type of aerophone found in African societies is the reed pipe. It is not, however, as widespread or as significant as the flute class. The single-reed type occurs in the savannah belt of west Africa, for example in Upper Volta, northern Ghana, Dahomey, and Chad, and is usually made out of the stalk of a millet or similar plant. The embouchure consists of a short flap about an inch in length and a quarter of an inch in diameter, made by cutting two parallel slits about two inches from one end of the stalk. The flap is not severed, but cut at one end so that it can be lifted with the hand, and is allowed to lie loosely over the embouchure; however, it may be held down by a loosely tied string. By exhaling and inhaling through the slits around the flap, one is able to get two distinct reedy sounds. The other end of the instrument may be cupped with the free hand to vary the pitch, or a fruit shell or calabash may be placed at one or both ends of the instrument.

We also find double-reed instruments, in Somalia, Chad, Cameroon, northern Nigeria, Upper Volta, and in eastern Africa along the coast of Kenya and Tanzania—areas with Islamic tradition.

Hausa double-reed pipe

Horns and Trumpets

Widespread use is made of animal horns and elephant tusks as trumpets, which are generally designed to be side-blown. Trumpets are also made out of whole lengths or composite sections of gourd, or a piece of small bamboo stem to which a bell made out of gourd is attached (see jacket photograph). Among the Lugbara of Uganda, the position of the gourd is reversed: the gourd, on which the embouchure is cut, is fixed as the mouthpiece. There are also trumpets made out of either bamboo or metal, such as the Ethiopian *malakat*, which may also be covered with leather or skin.

Trumpets made out of gourd or bamboo or both are usually end-blown, though side-blown varieties have also been noted.[2]

[2] See K. P. Wachsmann, "The Sound Instruments," 354.

Ensemble of ivory trumpets

Wooden trumpets in the form of human figures

End-blown trumpet with a gourd
affixed to the bell

There are both short and long trumpets of four to six feet, such as the *malakat* of Ethiopia and similar trumpets played by the Nyiramba and Nyisansu of Tanzania, by the Madi and Acholi of Uganda, and by some societies in the savannah belt of west Africa, particularly those that use double-reed instruments, such as the Hausa of northern Nigeria.

Trumpets are also carved out of wood, and are played by some societies in western, eastern, and central Africa; these are usually side-blown. Other varieties of wood trumpets played in vertical position, however, occur in Zaire. They have a headpiece of wood carved in the form of a human figure, below which the embouchure is cut.

Trumpets may be played singly, in pairs, or in larger ensembles, which are usually played hocket fashion, either alone or in combination with drums and other percussion. Horns and trumpets may be used for conveying signals and verbal messages as well as for playing music.

9 / Chordophones

Musical Bow

OF the variety of chordophones (string instruments) found in African societies, the musical bow appears to be the most widespread. It exists in a variety of forms, the simplest of which is the earth bow. This consists of a flexible stick stuck in the ground, to whose upper end a piece of string is attached. This string is stretched down and buried in the earth; a piece of stone may be placed on top of the earth to keep the string in position. In the places where it is found, such as northern Ghana and Uganda, it is usually regarded as a toy instrument.

Another simple type of bow is the mouth bow (a bow resonated in the mouth). A section of the bow's string—either close to the tip of the bow or towards the middle—is held across the mouth. As the bow is hit at a convenient spot, the shape and size of the mouth cavity are altered so as to amplify selected partials produced by the string. The vibrating string may be touched lightly by a stick or any convenient implement when the fundamental needs to be raised in pitch, and released for the tone of the open string.

In addition to mouth bows, there are bows with calabash resonators, placed in the middle of the bow or towards the tip. The string may be in one straight piece or it may be braced halfway to the middle of the bow, thus dividing it into two sections; some musical bows have as many as three such sections. When a bow with a calabash resonator is being played, the resonator may be placed on the chest or some part of the body when the fundamental pitch is being changed. Generally, no attempt is made to isolate and amplify specific partials, as in the technique of the mouth bow. The fundamental and the overtone sound together, and are heard as a chord.

In another type of musical bow, the emphasis is laid on the partials rather than on the fundamentals, for the latter are not sounded. The player isolates and uses the partials for melodic purposes. Instead of striking or plucking the string, he sets the string in motion by breathing in and out on a quill; the required pitches are selected and amplified in the mouth by varying the shape of the mouth cavity. The *gora* played in South Africa employs this technique. Another variant of this is the friction bow. It is a mouth bow whose bow stick is notched and rasped by a finely notched rattle stick. This friction activates the string of the bow, producing sympathetic vibrations.[1]

Southern Africa appears to be an area particularly rich in musical bows. P. R. Kirby lists about eight different varieties, although in terms of their acoustics they fall into the three categories described above.[2]

Zithers

Another type of chordophone found in African societies is the zither, whose distinguishing characteristic is the horizontal position of its strings. One variety is the idiochord zither, whose strings are made out of strands of the bark of the sticks that form

[1] For a description of this instrument and its music, see Thomas Johnson, "Xizambi Friction-bow Music of the Shangana-Tsonga," *African Music*, IV/4 (1970), 81–95.

[2] P. R. Kirby, *Musical Instruments of the Native Races of South Africa* (London, 1934).

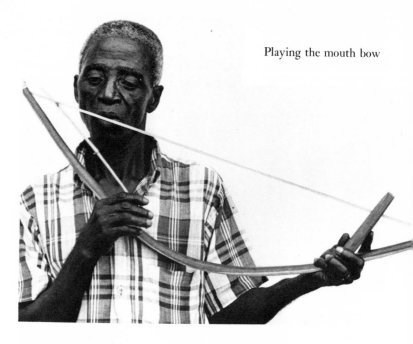

Playing the mouth bow

the frame of the instrument. A single piece of stick can be made in this manner into a monochord zither, care being taken not to remove the strand that forms the cord completely from the stick.

A number of such sticks (such as sticks cut out of the stalks of millet or a species of grass whose epidermis can be lifted with a knife) are put together and tied in the form of a raft to make a raft zither. The required pitch of each string can be obtained by ensuring that it has the right length and thickness, with adjustments in thickness made by wrapping each string with a separate cord. In some varieties of this instrument, each note has three sets of strings.

Another type of idiochord zither is the *mvet* of the Fang of Cameroons. About five feet of the rib of a rafia palm forms the base of this instrument. Separate strands of the frond are lifted with a knife to form the strings, and a gourd resonator is attached to the middle. Resonators of a smaller size may also be attached to each end.

Tube zithers are zithers whose strings run across the shell of a tube such as a hollow bamboo stem. The *valiha*, as this instrument

Trough zither

Five-string
bow zither

Raft zither

is called, is featured in performances by musical specialists; varieties of the *valiha* are found in different societies in Malagasy.[3]

Another type of African zither is the flat bar zither. It may have three or more strings stretched over frets carved on both sides of a flat bar. The bar is placed on edge, so that its flat side is sideways; the other end, which does not have a fret, rests on a gourd resonator tied to it. The strings of a zither may be mounted on a board or on a trough instead of a flat bar.

The bow zither is yet another variety, found in the savannah belt of west Africa, and consisting of a short U-shaped bow with a calabash resonator attached to its base. About five or six strings are tied from one side of the bow to the other. Each string is usually held down by a nut or screw made out of calabash or fish bone, or is simply wound around the stick. When played, it is held horizontally in front of the body.

Lutes

The lute, an instrument whose strings run parallel to its neck, is found in African societies in both bowed and plucked varieties. The most widespread of the former is the one-string fiddle, which appears in three main forms.

One type, found in Ethiopia, is the *masinko*, which resembles the spike fiddle (a lute with a spike fixed to the resonator, played vertically). The resonator, made of wood, is diamond-shaped and covered with goat skin. At important festivals, about fifteen to twenty of these may be played together.

Second, there is the one-string fiddle which has a family resemblance to the rebec, an Arabic version of the bowed lute. It has a wide distribution in the savannah belt of west Africa, where it is called the *riti* by the Wolof of Senegal, and the *goge*, *goje*, or *gonje* by the Hausa of Nigeria, the Songhai and Djerma of Niger, and the Dagomba of Ghana. It has a round or oval resonator, usually

[3] See photographs in album notes to *Musique Malgache* (Ocora, OCR 24), and Norma McLeod, "The Status of Musical Specialists in Madagascar," *Ethnomusicology*, VIII/3 (1964), 278–89.

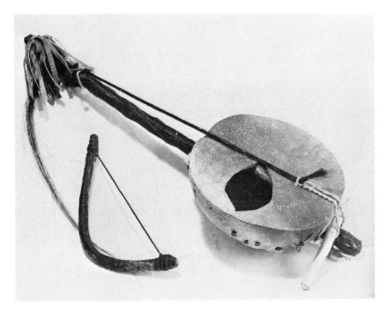

One-string fiddle

made of gourd or calabash, and is covered with the skin of the water lizard. The string is made out of a bundle of horse hair, the bow of similar material.

A third type of one-string fiddle is found in eastern and central Africa: the *sese* or *zeze* tube fiddle of Zaire, Kenya, and Tanzania, or the *endingidi* of Uganda. The resonator may be made out of gourd or a hollow piece of wood or bamboo, and covered with skin (such as that of the duiker). The string may be made out of sisal fiber and may be played with a bow of similar material.

Bowed lutes of two or four strings, which may be made out of gut, are also found in east Africa, among the Gogo of Tanzania. The two-string *zeze* may be played with a small, round piece of stick, while the four-string *zeze* is played with a bow of sisal fiber.

Plucked lutes show similar variations in form and size, as well as in the number of strings. They may have round resonators of gourd covered with skin, or elongated wooden resonators. They may be one-string lutes such as those played by the Songhai and Djerma of Niger, or instruments with two to five strings, such as the *khalam* of the Wolof of Senegambia.

Bow Lutes and Harp Lutes

All the lutes considered so far have straight necks, with the strings running parallel to the necks to which they are secured. However, two exceptions exist: one is the bow lute, in which the string is stretched from the tip of a bow to the resonator. A number of such bows, each carrying a string, may be fixed to a single resonator.

The other is the harp lute. A fairly straight neck is used, but instead of all the strings running parallel to the neck, they are passed over a perpendicular bridge with a number of notches on opposite sides. Each string is passed over a specific notch, the number of notches depending on the number of strings. The effect of the notch is to raise each string above the sounding board as it reaches the resonator. The number of strings may run from five or six to twenty-one; the most outstanding of these instruments is the twenty-one string *cora,* played in Guinea and Senegambia. Three different tunings are used for the *cora,* the choice depending on the piece to be played.

Harps

Closely related to the harp lute and the bow lute are arched (or bow) harps. The neck of the instrument is arched, and the strings run from the neck to the sound box at an angle. Thus, whereas the harp-lute has a straight neck, the bow harp has a curved neck, and does not use the notched bridge.

Varieties of the bow harp are found in the savannah belt of west Africa—in Guinea, Niger, northern Nigeria, Cameroon, Chad, and Gabon. The number of strings ranges from three (as in the *bolon* of the Malinke of Guinea) to ten (as in the *ngombi* bow lute of the Mbaka of Gabon.) East Africa is particularly rich in bow harps. Harps of five, six, seven, and eight strings are found in Uganda and Kenya.

A twenty-one-
string harp lute
(*cora*)

Playing a seven-string harp lute

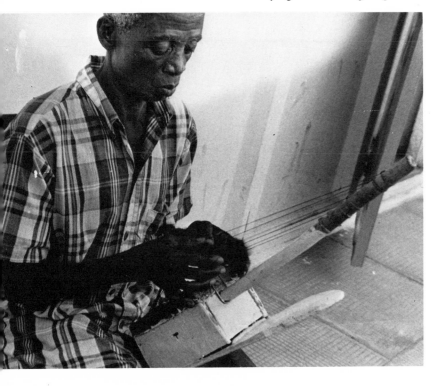

Bow harp from Zaire

Obukano lyre

Lyres

Unlike zithers, lutes, and harps, which are found in widely separated areas over the continent, the lyre, an instrument whose strings run from a yoke to a resonator, seems to be concentrated in east Africa. One very large type, the *begana*, occurs in Ethiopia. It has eight to twelve strings, and is primarily used during Lent and other festivals of the Ethiopian Church, although it may be played outside the church. The more popular lyre, the six-string *krar*, is considerably smaller than the *begana*.

There appear to be similar gradations in size in the Kenyan lyres. The *obukano*, a large variant, has been described as "the double bass of east Africa." It is three-and-a-half feet long, the resonating drum is eighteen inches in diameter, and the frame for the strings is thirty-one inches wide at the top. There are lyres of smaller size, such as the eight-string *litungu* of the Kuria of Kenya and the five-string *kibugander* of the Kipsigis of Kenya. According to Graham Hyslop, these instruments and others, like the *adeudeu* harp and the *siriri* bowed fiddle, are tuned in the baritone range.[4]

Uganda is also rich in lyres. The number of strings may vary from four or five (lyres of the Madi), to seven (lyres of Gishu people) or eight (lyres of the Ganda and the Soga). Lyres also occur in Zaire, among the Logo and Mabudu, as well as in the Sudan among, for example, the Shilluk, the Dinka, and the Nuer.[5]

Chordophones are particularly suitable for use as solo instruments. They may accompany solo singing or recitations of poetry, praise singing, and narrative songs. Examples of chordophone ensembles with other instruments are combinations of bowed lutes and rattles (Ghana, Upper Volta, Nigeria), bowed lute, lyre, drum, and rattle (Uganda), harp lutes and xylophones (Senegal), one to three lutes, tube zither, and rattle (Malagasy).

[4] Graham Hyslop, "African Musical Instruments in Kenya," *African Music*, II/1 (1958), 31–36.
[5] K. P. Wachsmann, "The Sound Instruments," 405.

SECTION THREE / *Structures in African Music*

10 / Organization of Instrumental Ensembles

THE structures used in African music represent usages which are learned through participation in musical events, passed on aurally from generation to generation, and applied, modified, and expanded by succeeding generations. They include melodic and rhythmic elements, both linear and multilinear, which permit limited improvisations to be made where appropriate.

An aspect of these structures that needs to be considered in relation to the music of the instruments reviewed in the preceding section is that of texture and density produced in instrumental combinations. Such combinations tend to follow definite patterns, for instruments are selected in relation to their effectiveness in performing certain established musical roles or for fulfilling specific musical purposes. While some instruments are designed for use as solo instruments, others are intended for use in ensembles. Within such groups, certain instruments function as lead or principal instruments, while others play a subordinate role as accompanying or ostinato instruments. Some instruments are used for enriching the texture of a piece of music or for increasing its density, while others emphasize its rhythmic aspects or articulate its pulse structure.

Moreover, since the African concept of a musical sound gives equal prominence to sounds of indefinite as well as definite pitch, instrumental combinations reflect this, being formed out of instruments of either or both categories. Accordingly, instrumental combinations that are meaningful in terms of the aesthetics of African music fall into three main categories.

First, ensembles may consist exclusively of melodic instruments (instruments of definite pitch). These are used in homogeneous groups or sometimes in mixed combinations of two or three instrumental types—flute ensembles, trumpet ensembles, combined ensembles of flutes and trumpets, combinations of bowed and plucked lutes or harp lutes and plucked lutes, of harp lutes and xylophones, or of lutes and lyres. With the exception of combinations with tuned idiophones, the music of such ensembles generally lacks the clear external definition of pulse structure one finds in other combinations. Such ensembles are accordingly used in contexts in which the absence of an articulated time line (see pp. 126, 131) is not felt as a deficiency.

The second category of instrumental combination includes ensembles of instruments capable only of indefinite pitches, such as drums, bells, rattles, stick clappers, etc. Some possibilities are homogeneous groups of single drum types, such as ensembles of wooden slit drums, hourglass tension drums, single-headed gourd drums, or double-headed drums, as well as mixed ensembles of different types of drums. The latter are usually composed of sets of varying sonorities, and may include a high-pitched drum, a medium-pitched drum, a tenor drum, and a low-pitched drum. Any two or three of these may be combined, provided they show enough contrast in sonority for one to emerge as the principal instrument and the others as accompaniment. Generally, it is the lowest-pitched drum that acts as the dominant (master) drum. Ensembles of drums may be played alone or in combination with one or two bells, one or more rattles, stick clappers, etc., depending on the range of intensity and tone contrasts desired. In addition, some of these instruments may be used for articulating the pulse structure of the music, i.e., providing a time line. The use of the sounds of drums and other percussive instruments of indefinite pitches as a basis for music in their own right encourages the organization of extraneous sounds into some sort of music in work situations. This invites making music with improvised sound-producing objects such as blades of hoes, oars, tins, packing cases, or implements

Drum ensemble accompanied by a double bell

used for pounding grain or beating the floors of newly built houses.

The combination of both melodic and percussive instruments is the third type of instrumental ensemble. This includes groups of flutes and drums, of flutes, drums, and bells, and of xylophones, rattles, percussion sticks, and membranophones, etc. As such combinations give scope to both rhythmic and melodic functions, they are much more prevalent than combinations featuring only melodic instruments.

By extension, solo performers may also combine melodic and rhythmic characteristics. When the player of a musical bow strikes the cord of the bow with a piece of stick, he achieves a percussive effect. A Shangana Tsonga musician adds a percussive texture to his music by rasping the notched stick of his musical bow with the notched handle of a fruit shell rattle.[1] The player of the *obukhana* (an eight-string lyre of the Elgon area of Kenya, smaller

[1] Thomas Johnson, "Xizambi Friction-bow Music of the Shangana-Tsonga," 81–95.

Ensemble of xylophones and drums

and higher-pitched than the *litungu*) provides a percussive accompaniment by tapping a metal ring worn on the big toe of his right foot against the frame of his instrument, while activating ankle bells worn on the same foot. Similarly, the player of the Kuria *litungu* (eight-string lyre) accompanies his music with a percussion instrument "held between the big toe of his right foot and the next one to it," which he strikes against the lower frame of his instrument. The lyre is placed on the ground on its side. The percussion instrument, according to Graham Hyslop, "consists of a large pea-pod shaped bell." [2]

Another way of achieving percussive effects is by tapping the side of a resonator or rasping the skin stretched over it. The player of the Konkomba plucked lute rasps the skin in this manner with

[2] Graham Hyslop, "Some Musical Instruments of Kenya," *African Arts*, V/4 (1972), 54.

his fingers or finger nails. So does the Teso player of the *adeudeu* five-string harp, using the fingers of one hand "to snap out a percussion figure on the drum like tip of the bowl sound box." [3]

Some solo performers achieve similar effects by asking other people to play a rattle, a bell, or some such idiophone for them. A Dagomba, Frafra, or Hausa bowed lute player always has one or two rattle players to assist him. Similarly, a Lobi-Dagarti xylophonist may be assisted by a second person who reinforces the tune with the right hand while he hits the edge of the lowest key with the hard end of the beater held in the left hand; for the full complement of percussive sounds, he would find supporting drummers. Similarly, the player of the *litungu* lyre of Bukusu country in Kenya is accompanied by someone who plays a percussion stick. Sometimes percussion and melodic instruments are even played in alternation by the same performers. Some societies make "whistle drum sticks" so that they can use one end of the instrument for drumming and the other end for playing melodic interludes.

It would seem, therefore, that an examination of the aesthetics of African music reveals a distinct bias toward percussion and the use of percussive techniques, not only because of the structural functions of such instruments, but also because of a preference for musical textures that embody percussive sounds or sounds that increase the ratio of noise to pitch.

[3] Ibid., 52.

11 / Melody and Polyphony in Instrumental Music

THE scales on which instrumental melodies are based usually have between four and seven steps, with the choice of these steps depending entirely on the individual society and culture. Within each tradition, some instruments may have only a few of the tones of the scale, some may cover the whole octave, and others may cover one to three octaves. In instruments of fixed pitches such as xylophones, the steps of the scale are arranged progressively from low to high; but there are others in which the steps are arranged in sequences related to the structure of melodic patterns.

The constituent tones of a scale are not always represented on an instrument. In some cases, only a basic tuning is given, and the performer must apply appropriate techniques to produce the rest of the notes of the melody. For example, the pitch of a one-string fiddle in the open string position is modified by appropriate fingering. A Gogo two-string bowed lute is tuned in a minor third; the higher-pitched string produces the rest of the notes of the scale through the use of appropriate fingering. Similarly, there are flutes whose pitch ranges are extended by overblowing: the Bashi *mulizi*, for example, has two finger holes, but it can be made to play three octaves of a heptatonic (seven-tone) scale through the use of appropriate playing techniques.[1] In the *mbeta* flute ensemble of the

[1] A. P. Merriam, "Musical Instruments and Techniques of Performance among the Bashi," *Zaire*, IX/2 (1955), 121–32.

Luguru of Tanzania, the person who plays the lowest flute in the set extends the single tone of his instrument down by singing two additional tones of the scale whenever these are required.

The actual pitches of the basic scale steps show considerable variation from one society to another; sometimes such variations are found even within the same culture—that is why the Lobi of Ghana maintain that those who wish to play xylophones together should obtain them from the same instrument maker. Moreover, it appears that some traditions lean towards equidistant tuning, while others maintain nonequidistant tuning. (A tuning can be said to be equidistant when the intervals between tones are approximately the same.)

Apart from the question of intonation or pitch realizations, the note arrangements of four-, five-, and six-step tunings emerge in different forms. Example XI–1 below shows some of the varieties of four-step (tetratonic) tunings. They have been written out in four groups according to the intervallic patterns they display, which characterize the melodies based on them: [2]

Type A includes typical intervals that are approximately major seconds, thirds, fourths, and fifths.

Type B is characterized by the presence of a half tone or something close to a minor second.

Type C is characterized by the presence of augmented or diminished fourths.

Type D is an equidistant pattern.

---

[2] The conventional staff notation has been used for notating all the music examples in this work, since this system will be familiar to most readers. Notated pitches are approximate, and do not have the exact values of those of the Western tempered scale. In songs in strict time, the barline is used in accordance with current African practice for indicating regular divisions of the time span (see page 126), and not for indicating shifts of melodic accents.

Example XI–1

Five-tone (pentatonic) scales are found in both equidistant and nonequidistant forms. Each step of an ideal equidistant scale is larger than a major second but less than a minor third. Nonequidistant five-tone scales occur in two major types: the pentatonic without a half step (the anhemitonic pentatonic, Example XI–2, a) and the pentatonic with one or two half steps (the hemitonic pentatonic, Example XI–2, b).

Example XI–2

a. Anhemitonic Pentatonic Forms

b. Hemitonic Pentatonic Forms

Six-tone (hexatonic) scales also occur in equidistant and nonequidistant forms. An equidistant hexatonic scale would be a whole-tone scale, while a nonequidistant hexatonic scale would include a semitone, as in the examples below:

Example XI–3 *Nonequidistant Hexatonic*

Seven-tone (heptatonic) scales are the simplest of all the scale types, and also occur in equidistant and nonequidistant forms. The latter incorporates semitones, whole tones, and intervals which are slightly less than a whole tone or slightly larger than a semitone, especially between the third and fourth degrees and the seventh and eighth degrees.

Example XI–4

More complex scale patterns are also found here and there, particularly in instrumental music, as in Example XI–5 below noted by Henry Weman [3], which includes chromatic segments. It is the tuning of an *mbira* of a Karanga player from the Musume district of Rhodesia.

Example XI–5

Instrumental Melodies

Instrumental tunes constructed out of the above scales may take three forms. First, instrumental pieces may follow the formal structure of songs, making use of the melodic intervals, contours, and phrases characteristic of the particular vocal tradition. Some instrumental pieces originate as songs with words, though variations of the materials of the basic tune may be introduced during a performance. Where the instrumental form and technique allow— as in the music of the twenty-one-string *cora*—a few decorative figures and short runs may be used; [4] but the piece remains an essen-

---

[3] Henry Weman, *African Music and Church in Africa* (Uppsala, 1960), 40.

[4] For a study of the music of this instrument see Roderick Knight, *An Analytical Study of Music for the Kora, a West African Harp Lute*, M. A. thesis, University of California at Los Angeles, 1968.

tially lyrical one, an instrumental version of vocal melodies.

In the second type of melodic formation, instrumental tunes are arranged as sequences of repeated melodic patterns or figures. The use of these patterns may be determined by the layout of the keys or strings of the instrument, as, for example, in the performance of *mbira* music or the music of lyres and bow harps whose strings are tuned in functional groups.

Example XI–6: *Layout of the Keys of the Mbira, and the Resulting Melodic Sequence*

The use of repeated melodic patterns seems unavoidable in instruments with a limited range of two or three tones that can therefore not cope with the ordinary contour of songs. This design of repeated melodic figures seems ideal for accompanying songs or for providing a continuum for poetic recitations. Some instruments in the aerophone family are not suitable for playing even such limited melodic patterns. Hence, some of them are used merely for producing rhythmic or textural effects, while others are graded in pitch so that they can be played hocket fashion, with each instrument contributing its pitch at the appropriate point in the melody, pattern, or figure.

The third type of melodic formation attempts to achieve the combined effect of a songlike melody or figure by a method of linear elaboration which increases the density of the sound events. The melody or figure, distributed to both hands, is played in interlocking fashion so that each note is repeated or followed by a different note that continues the melodic chain. This technique forms the basis of the design of the music of chordophones like harps and lyres of Uganda and southern Sudan, as well as the *mbira* and xylophone music of those areas. Example XI–7 illustrates this man-

ner of elaboration which results in a new tune as the mind links the
successive tones into a different pattern.

Example XI–7 [5]

A limited extension of this design occurs in *mbira* music.
Here, some keys are played in linear sequence, while others are
plucked together. Auxiliary notes may be played simultaneously
with notes of the melodic nucleus or as passing notes, in order to
provide some elaboration of the basic melody.

Example XI–8 [6]

[5] Gerhard Kubik, "Ennanga Music," *African Music,* IV/1 (1966/67), 23.
[6] From Andrew Tracey, "Three Tunes on the Mbira Dza Vadzimu," 25.

Instrumental Polyphony

Limited manifestations of polyphony (many-voiced or multipart music) occur in African instrumental traditions. In one possibility, the parts are arranged so that some of the tones of the contrasting parts are sounded simultaneously with the main part, while others are sounded separately. This is the organization of some aerophone ensembles employing the hocket technique, as in the extract below.

Example XI–9

The technique of *mbira* music of the Shona and other societies of Rhodesia also employs this organization to a large extent. A series of two-note chords (each of which may be struck simultaneously or treated as a broken chord) is used as a framework for the organization of the sound material.[7]

Example XI–10

[7] For studies of this music, see Andrew Tracey, "Mbira Music of Jege A. Tapera," "Three Tunes on the Mbira Dza Vadzimu," and "The Matepe Mbira Music of Rhodesia."

Chordal patterns also occur in music played on the musical bow, but these arise from the particular choice of partials selected for amplification along with the fundamental.[8]

Example XI-11

In societies that use seven-tone scales, homophonic polyphony in instrumental music is based on parallel thirds and sixths, and passing intervals of sevenths, fifths, and fourths.

Polyphony of a more contrapuntal nature is also exploited. This may take the form of simultaneous melodies, melody and supporting ostinato or ostinati, or interlocking melodic figures. In Malinke xylophone music, for example, the leader plays the main tune and the improvised parts, while the other player or players provide the accompanying melodic patterns. Similarly, in the xylophone music of the Chopi, each of the three or four supporting sets of xylophones plays an ostinato pattern in support of the main melody, while the leader plays improvised variations.[9]

In Lobi xylophone music, the right hand generally plays the main melody while the left hand accompanies it with a figure based on a counter-rhythm. Polyphony of a more contrapuntal nature is also exploited, taking the form of simultaneous melodies, melody and supporting ostinato or ostinati (Example XI-12), or interlocking melodic figures (Example XI-13).

[8] For a study of the music of musical bows, see David Rycroft, "Friction Chordophones in South Eastern Africa," *The Galpin Society Journal*, XIX (1966), 84–100.

[9] See Hugh Tracey, *Chopi Musicians: Their Music, Poetry and Instruments.*

Example XI–12

Example XI–13 [10]

Polyphonic design of a rather high density is used by the Ganda in some of their instrumental combinations. In *ndongo* music, for example, the tune is begun by the lyre player, followed by the fiddle player, who plays an elaboration of it while the lyre player improvises on it; a percussion section comes in soon after the two chordophones. To these, one more layer is added—the vocal line.

[10] Atta A. Mensah, "The Polyphony of Gyil-gu, Kudzo and Awutu Sakumo," *Journal of the International Folk Music Council,* XIX (1967), 76.

12 / The Rhythmic Basis of Instrumental Music

THE melodic and polyphonic forms utilized in African music derive their dynamic qualities from the rhythmic framework within which sound materials are organized. African traditions are more uniform in their choice and use of rhythms and rhythmic structures than they are in their selection and use of pitch systems. Since African music is predisposed towards percussion and percussive textures, there is an understandable emphasis on rhythm, for rhythmic interest often compensates for the absence of melody or the lack of melodic sophistication. The music of an instrument with a range of only two or three tones may be effective or aesthetically satisfying to its performers and their audience if it has sufficient rhythmic interest.

Instrumental rhythms are organized in both linear and multi-linear forms, and are generally conceived of either as syllabic rhythms reflecting those of songs, or as abstract rhythm patterns. The latter are used as a basis of melodic figures played by melodic instruments, as rhythmic figures which may be combined in a percussion piece, or as ostinati. The syllabic rhythms are used in lyrical instrumental style, and may be grouped in variable phrases corresponding to those of songs. They may be metrically free and lacking in rhythmical regularity, or they may be in strict time, imparting a feeling of regularity of beat which can be articulated in regular bodily movement.

The interrelationship of rhythmic patterns or phrases in strict time is controlled by relating them to a fixed *time span*, which can be broken up into an equal number of segments or pulses of different densities. It can be divided into:

A. *Two and multiples of two:* two, four, eight, or sixteen pulses, as shown below.

Example XII–1

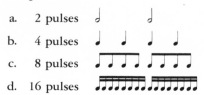

a. 2 pulses

b. 4 pulses

c. 8 pulses

d. 16 pulses

B. *Three and multiples of three:* three, six, twelve, or twenty-four pulses, as shown below.

Example XII–2

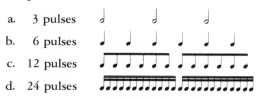

a. 3 pulses

b. 6 pulses

c. 12 pulses

d. 24 pulses

From the foregoing tables, it will be obvious that the greater the number of divisions, the greater the density of pulse; the fewer the number of divisions, the lower the density of pulse. In terms of rhythmic motion, therefore, we may infer that at any given tempo, the greater the number of divisions or pulses, the faster the rhythmic motion; the fewer the number, the slower the motion. Hence, in each of the two schemes of pulse structure, (a) represents slow pulse and (b) moderate pulse, while (c) represents fast pulse and (d) the fastest pulse.

Generally, it is the moderate pulse (b) that is articulated in hand clapping or externalized in the beat of a simple idiophone like a stick clapper or a castanet. It can therefore be regarded as the basic pulse that guides performers. Sometimes the slow pulse (a) is used for the same purpose. The pulses that have a high density (c and d) constitute the basis for melodic and percussion rhythms. They have therefore been designated as basic unit of structure, or *density referent.*

It is important to note that, although the schemes of pulse structure in **A** (two and multiples of two) and **B** (three and multiples of three) are different, the time span is the same in both cases. The pulses in **A** and **B** are, therefore, in a ratio of 2 to 3, as shown below.

Example XII–3

Bearing these relationships in mind, we can refer to rhythms based on pulse structure **A** as *duple rhythm* and those based on **B** as *triple rhythm*, using the terms duple and triple merely to refer to the underlying scheme of pulse structure.

The regular divisions of the time span do not always occur in duple or triple forms, however. They are also conceived of in terms of alternating sections of duple and triple; that is, a linear realization of the ratio 2:3, as shown below.

Example XII–4

This pulse structure is referred to as a *hemiola*. It is a combination of two equal sections of duple and triple; each section may have further subdivisions.

Example XII–5

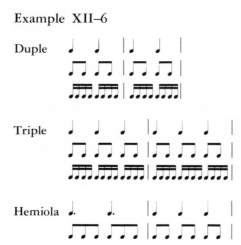

Formation of Rhythmic Patterns

The rhythmic patterns formed on the basis of the foregoing schemes of pulse structure are of two types: divisive and additive. *Divisive rhythms* are those that articulate the regular divisions of the time span, rhythms that follow the scheme of pulse structure in the grouping of notes. They may follow the duple, triple, or hemiola schemes, as shown below.

Example XII–6

Divisive rhythms may also be built out of combinations of different pulse structures. The patterns are usually in two contrasting sections, e.g.,

Example XII–7

a.

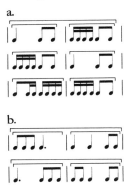

b.

The sections combined to form rhythmic patterns can be set out in tabular form, as shown in Example XII–8 on page 130.

While divisive rhythms follow the internal divisions of the time span, *additive rhythms* do not. The durational values of some notes may extend beyond the regular divisions within the time span. Instead of note groups or sections of the same length, different groups are combined within the time span. That is, instead of a phrase of twelve pulses being divided into 6 + 6, it may be divided onto 7 + 5 or 5 + 7.

Example XII–9

Example XII–8

a.

b.

Similarly, in duple rhythm, a phrase of eight pulses may be divided into 5 + 3 or 3 + 5, or into 3 + 2 + 3, 2 + 3 + 3, or 3 + 3 + 2.

Example XII–10

The use of additive rhythms in duple, triple, and hemiola patterns is the hallmark of rhythmic organization in African music, which finds its highest expression in percussion music.

It remains to point out that the length of rhythmic phrases is not always confined to the boundaries of the time span, but may be shorter or longer. For this reason, the time span acts at once as a measure and a standard phrase length to which rhythmic phrases are related. A performer must learn to keep the initial pulse of the time span—the regulative beat or the basic pulse—subjectively, while playing divisive and additive rhythms in phrases of different lengths. The listener or dancer must also be able to discover the regulative beat or basic pulse from the rhythmic structure that emerges in the performance.

The Time Line

Because of the difficulty of keeping subjective metronomic time in this manner, African traditions facilitate this process by externalizing the basic pulse. As already noted, this may be shown through hand clapping or through the beats of a simple idiophone. The guideline which is related to the time span in this manner has come to be described as a *time line*.

Because the time line is sounded as part of the music, it is regarded as an accompanying rhythm and a means by which rhythmic motion is sustained. Hence, instead of a time line that represents simple regular beats reflecting the basic pulse, a more complex form may be used. It may be designed as a rhythmic pattern in additive or divisive form, embodying the basic pulse or regulative beat as well as the density referent. Instead of a regular group of four notes, groups of five, six, and seven notes may be used in duple or triple rhythmic patterns.

Example XII–11

a. Duple rhythm

b. Triple rhythm

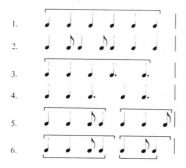

Multilinear Rhythms

The regular use of a time line as an accompanying rhythm shows that the use of multipart rhythmic structures is quite normal in African musical practice. Instead of a single accompanying idiophone, a number of such instruments may be put together in the rhythm section, and each one may reinforce the basic pulse in a particular way. When another instrument such as a drum is added to the rhythm section, this may also be assigned a different rhythmic part.

Multilinear rhythmic organization finds its highest expression in the music of percussion or in the percussive section of aerophone and chordophone ensembles. It follows well-established principles and procedures, one of which is the principle of *grading*. The rhythms to be combined in this manner must be graded in density or complexity in relation to the role of each part as accompanying, response, or lead instrument. Instruments which perform similar roles may have a similar degree of complexity.

Example XII–12: *Grading*

1.

2.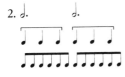

3.

Another important principle is that of *spacing*. Here, the rhythmic lines may be organized in such a way that they interlock. In order to achieve this, the parts which interlock are arranged so that they start at different but specified points in time.

Example XII–13: *Spacing*

The interlocking parts may be arranged in such a way that by their overlapping they form a resultant pattern. Alternatively, the interlocking parts may be exactly the same rhythm spaced differently, thereby creating a greater density of sounds.

Example XII–14

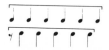

Contrasts in the tones of the interlocking parts similarly form a pattern heard as a resultant, which is, in effect, the realization of a preconceived figure, theme, or tune. Hence, it is this resultant that forms the basis of the initial organization of the parts.

Two types of rhythmic effects emerge from these procedures, one of which is *cross rhythm*. This interplay arises where rhythms based on different schemes of pulse structure are juxtaposed. The simplest type of cross rhythm is that based on the ratio of two against three, or their multiples—that is, *vertical* interplay of duple and triple rhythms (as opposed to hemiola, where the interplay is linear).

Example XII–15

More complex cross rhythms result when divisive and additive rhythms are juxtaposed.

Example XII–16

The spacing of rhythmic patterns in terms of points of entry produces the second effect, the *interplay of polyrhythms*. As the spacing of such rhythms is guided by the resultant figure or tune expected to emerge out of the interplay, it is important that the entry points are not missed, since this will cause confusion of the expected resultant.

Both cross rhythms and polyrhythms may sometimes be handled by one and the same performer when he pits the left hand against the right hand. Every good drummer learns to handle these as he masters the techniques of drumming. Generally, the rhythms are approached from the resultant, from which patterns forming coherent wholes are abstracted and assigned to each hand, as in the example that follows:

Example XII–17

Resultant Pattern	♪♩ ♪♩ ♫♫ ♪♩
Right Hand	♩. ♩. ♩ ♪♩.
Left Hand	♪ ♩ ♪ ♩ ♪ ♩ ♪ ♩

A lot depends on the conception of the basic theme or tune and the contrasts that it embodies, for these factors determine how the parts should be disposed and coordinated. The same sort of effect can, of course, be produced by two players, one playing the right-hand pattern and the other, the left-hand pattern.

From the point of view of execution, polyrhythmic design is always the most difficult for the inexperienced performer, because it demands that the performer maintain an independent part while relating himself in terms of spacing to the time line or to other performers. The feeling of a rhythmic pattern played in isolation is never the same as when that pattern is played in some position within a time line, or when it has to be related to some other rhythm with which it produces a resultant.

It must also be noted that the same rhythmic pattern can be placed in different positions in relation to the time line. It may start at the beginning, in the middle, or in various positions after the start or the midpoint, depending on the desired resultant.

The crucial point in polyrhythmic procedures, therefore, is the spacing or the placement of rhythmic patterns that are related to one another at different points in time so as to produce the anticipated integrated structure. In this connection, what has been described as offbeat phrasing will be seen as a favorite procedure in polyrhythmic organization.

Example XII–18

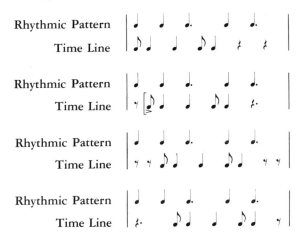

It must further be pointed out that the parts of all the instruments of an ensemble need not always be arranged polyrhythmically. Some may have the same beginning point and show internal contrasts through the use of cross rhythms, while others begin at different points. A great deal depends on how the music is conceived and on the breadth and variety of movements to which it is related. Moreover, in both linear and multilinear structures, rhythmic organization gains in clarity when it is arranged within a framework of contrasting pitches. In linear organization, the use of the different pitches of a single instrument as a framework allows for the same rhythmic pattern to be varied in several ways, e.g.,

Example XII–19

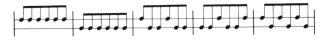

In multilinear organization, the use of instruments of different pitches and timbres enables each one to be distinctly heard. It enables their cross rhythms to stand out clearly in the form of little

"tunes." Hence, although rhythm is the primary focus in drumming, some attention is paid to pitch level, for the aesthetic appeal of drumming lies in the organization of the rhythmic and melodic elements.

It is for similar reasons of design that attempts are made to utilize sonority contrasts wherever possible, even in the parts played by idiophones. The tones produced by shaking a rattle may be varied by hitting the instrument against the body or the palm, or by slapping it with the fingers. Similarly, a stamping tube may be played in such a way as to produce sonority contrasts which can be exploited in the formation of rhythmic patterns.

13 / Organization of Vocal Music

ALTHOUGH the cultivation of music performed on instruments receives attention in African musical traditions, instrumental music is not regarded everywhere as something that should be developed in its own right. Many traditions have a tendency to combine it with some singing, either by other performers or by the instrumentalists themselves. Players of chordophones are often singers as well, while the art of the *mbira* performer lies not only in the formation of chordal sequences and melodic patterns, but also in the appropriate use of vocal tones, melodic phrases, or complete songs. Xylophones may be played alone or combined with a chorus; likewise, combinations of flutes and chorus or drums and chorus abound. In all such combinations with voice, the actual role of the vocal part or its importance in the design of the music is variable. It may be subordinate to the instrumental part, or it may be of equal or greater importance, depending on the context and function of the music.

It must also be noted that vocal music is cultivated everywhere in its own right, both as a group activity and as a means of individual expression. In some societies, individual singing forms part of institutionalized behavior; among the Karimojong and other pastoral societies of eastern Africa, for example, the composition and performance of individual songs on social occasions is quite a normal practice.[1]

The vocal forms used in African societies, therefore, include accompanied and unaccompanied solos, songs performed by two people in unison or in a duet, and songs performed by choruses.

Organization of Solo Singing

Solos may be organized either in strophic form (a single verse repeated, often with slight variations, for the desired number of stanzas), or in the form of a series of declamations or cumulative nonstanzaic utterances, possibly rounded off by closing refrains or pauses. In accompanied solos, the gap between declamations or strophes may be bridged by the accompanying instrument; an arrangement in which the voice and the instrument work in alternation, in a call-and-response pattern, is also possible. When the latter is used, the performer may play a few notes or tap an accompanying rhythm on the resonator of his instrument while singing. Some African traditions have additional forms of solo singing which require accompaniment by a chorus that chimes in at appropriate points or sings special responses. This, however, does not seem to be widely exploited.

Organization of Group Singing

Songs intended to be sung by two people in a kind of duet or by four people singing antiphonally in pairs are found in at least three standard forms. The first is a simple call-and-response or similar form, in which the second singer echoes every musical phrase sung by the first, possibly with a closing refrain rounding off a number of these alternations. Another arrangement provides for a brief lead of a few notes by one of the singers, the second joining in as soon as possible to sing along with him to the end of the

---

[1] See K. A. Gourlay, "The Making of Karimojong Cattle Songs," *Mila: A Biannual Newsletter of Cultural Research,* II/1 (1971), 34–48.

section. In the third form, both singers begin simultaneously and sing each stanza together.

Pieces intended to be sung by choruses are generally designed for a lead singer or cantor, or for a group of lead singers and a chorus. The simplest form is the one in which the lead singer sings an entire verse through, repeated immediately by the chorus.

Other songs are organized into clear sections for a lead singer and a chorus. In the simplest type, each section consists of a single phrase, sung by the lead singer and answered by the chorus with a set response. This response phrase may be similar to the lead phrase (Example XIII–1) or it may be a continuation of it (Example XIII–2).

Example XIII–1

Example XIII–2

Substantial variations in the lead section—for example, differences arising from significant changes in the text—may also be reflected in the choral response. However, there are songs in which the response section remains virtually the same while the call phrases change, giving rise to the form A–B–C–B (as in Example XIII–1 above). Other pieces are designed in such a way that both sections change, giving rise to the form A–B–C–D, where A and C are sung by cantor and B and D by the chorus. When such a series forms a strophe, the entire formal scheme is repeated for each succeeding strophe.

Alternating phrases by cantor and chorus may be juxtaposed, or they may overlap. In the latter case, it is usually the lead singer who overlaps with the chorus by starting his solo before each chorus response ends:

Example XIII–3

In addition, a series of alternating call-and-response phrases may be rounded off with a concluding section or refrain sung by both cantor and chorus. Sometimes the entire series may be preceded by an introductory section as well, sung by the lead singer or by two or more lead singers singing one after the other. It is also possible for a lead singer to go back once or twice to the introduction or to similar material after the first chorus entry, before concentrating on the main alternating phrase section.

Other variants of the call-and-response form provide long sections for either the cantor or the chorus:

Example XIII–4

Where a cantor's solo section is long, he exercises the option to eliminate some of the repeats, and bring in the chorus sooner. The chorus, on the other hand, has no such freedom, and cannot curtail its response without the intervention of the cantor.

A chorus response can be interrupted by a cantor where the song lends itself to the use of this technique. The cantor chooses a convenient point before the end of a response phrase and introduces a new lead phrase; the chorus stops singing as soon as they hear him, picking up the response again when he gives them a cue, which is implied in the way he ends his phrase. (This differs from the standard overlapping call-and-response technique.) In order to remind the chorus of the correct response or to draw their attention to the particular song that has been started, a cantor may begin with the response phrase and then go on to his lead section.

Not all African societies organize their choral singing along the lines described above; some have more elaborate forms. For example, a Masai chorus may be organized in three parts: one for the lead singer, one for the chorus that responds to the lead sections, and an ostinato, which is sung by another group against the alternating call-and-response phrases. The choral style of the Giriama of Kenya or the Ekonda of Zaire is based on a multipart structure which allows for two or three people to sing the call section together in parts, and for the chorus to respond similarly in parts. Both sections may also overlap, giving rise to a complex texture.[2]

Another form of complex choral organization is used by the Nguni-speaking peoples of South Africa. At least two voice parts form the basis of this style, and each part may carry its own text. The parts do not begin simultaneously or operate in alternation; rather, each one makes an independent entry, giving rise to constant overlapping of their phrases. When other voices are added, some of them may run counter to the two main parts, while others

Example XIII–5 [3]

[2] See A. P. Merriam, *Ekonda: Tribal Music of the Belgian Congo*, album notes (Riverside RLP-4006).

[3] Nicholas England, "Bushman Counterpoint," *Journal of the International Folk Music Council*, XIX (1967), 62.

double them. The result is an intricate vocal texture in which individual voices enter and re-enter at different points, singing nonidentical texts.[4]

Another type of involved choral organization is used by the Bushmen. A basic phrase design that forms the framework of a song is elaborated simultaneously by individual singers who insert tones and shorten or prolong rhythmic values until they arrive at a melody that pleases them, which is then repeated in a complex polyphonic form with suitable variations (Example XIII–5).

Canonic singing is employed as well, for example, by the Bushmen, the Shona of Rhodesia, and the Jabo of Liberia.

Example XIII–6 [5]

The preferred voice qualities for songs intended to be performed by individuals and groups are not dictated by uniform stan-

[4] See David Rycroft, "Nguni Vocal Polyphony," *Journal of the International Folk Music Council*, XIX (1967), 88–103.

[5] Robert A. Kauffman, *Multi-part Relationships in the Shona Music of Rhodesia*, Ph.D. dissertation, University of California at Los Angeles, 1970.

dards. Some traditions emphasize open voice quality, while others favor a more constricted sound. Occasionally one finds the use of falsetto or high tessitura, deliberate use of yodelling, humming or even whispering in specific contexts (as in the vocal accompaniment to Sandawe music for the trough zither), the use of rising attack and falling release, the presence or absence of vibrato in specific structural contexts, or tremolo caused by the deliberate use of tongue flutter. Some societies begin their singing with a loud outburst which diminishes suddenly or gradually towards the end of the phrase, while others maintain a fairly even dynamic level.

14 / Melody and Polyphony in Vocal Music

THE scales used in vocal music, having from four to seven steps, are not unlike those used in instrumental music. For any given scale step, however, one may not always find absolute correspondence between the vocal pitches and the instrumental tunings. In African musical practice, the areas of tolerance of pitch variation for particular steps of the scale are much larger than those of traditions that base their music on a fixed pitch of 440 vibrations per second for A.

The structure of melodies built out of these scales is based on the controlled use of selected interval sequences. Thinking in terms of these sequences, which reflect melodic processes rather than the scales as contructs, gives one greater insight into the usages that guide perfomers, for the patterns formed by these sequences are used in creating new songs or for varying existing materials when the situation demands it. From this point of view, five types of melodic structures related to scale types need to be distinguished.

First, there are structures that limit the melodic line to the use of two basic descending intervals of a fourth (C′–G–D or A–E–B), or its inversion, with octave duplications possible as well (Example XIV–1, A). Melodies employing this structure are essentially

Example XIV-1

tritonic. Thus, instead of C′–G–D or A′–E′–B, one may have D′–C′–G–D–C or B′–A′–E′–B–A, as in the song quoted in Example XIV–2. In this structure, therefore, no intervals other than seconds and fourths or their inversions are possible.

Example XIV-2 [1]

[1] David Rycroft, "Zulu and Xhosa Praise Poetry and Song," *African Music,* III/1 (1962), 81.

be - ka nyan - gan - ye bam khiph - i___ le
le U - se gug il' u - ba - ba U - se gug___ i - le

The second type of structure limits the melodic line to three sequences of thirds, or to two consecutive thirds and a second (Example XIV–1, B). The melodies based on this structure may also include fourths, fifths, or sixths in restricted positions: for example, C–G (fifth), E–A, and G–C′ (fourths).

Example XIV–3

In the third type of scale formation, the melodic line is limited to the use of only two sequences of seconds or thirds (Example XIV–1, C). In such melodies, conjunct movement (movement in seconds) is limited to the trichord, that is, to two sequences of major seconds. Within the phrase, a trichord must be followed by an interval larger than a second. Melodies based on this structure can have two sequences of thirds. The melodic progression usually requires that such sequences be followed by an interval smaller or larger than a third: that is, by a second or a fourth (Example XIV–3). In addition to the trichordal sequence and the use of two consecutive thirds, other intervals such as the octave, the fifth, and the fourth occur. Inversions of the second and third are used where the vocal style exploits melodic leaps. The following songs illustrate features of melodic organization based on this structure.

Example XIV–4

a.

H5 - le-lee__ H5 - le - lee, H5 - le -lee____ E-nya ya mie gblɔ ɖoě - te fe vɔ, H5 - le - lee__ H5 - le - lee

b.

A-na wo wu ee___ ye wo__ dui a a-gbe. Ee___ a na wo wu ee ye wo__ dui a a-gbe ee.

Slight modification of the interval structures used in the above occurs in some traditions: instead of a major sixth, a minor seventh is used. That is, instead of C–D–E–G–A, we have C–D–E–G–B♭ (see Example XIV–1, C, last formation); this gives a distinctive character to the music.

An important feature of melodic organization associated with pentatonic structures is that of transposition, whereby the melody is shifted from one position of a trichord to another. The shift may be a whole step, or as much as two or three steps, up or down. That is, there could be a shift from a G–A–B or E–G–A–B sequence to an F–G–A or D–F–G–A sequence within the same song, or from A–G–F to D′–C–B♭ in the same song.

The songs below illustrate this. In Example XIV–5, the notes E and F never occur in sequence as E–F, since this would change the structure of the piece.

Example XIV–5

Ta a - vɔ na le - gba, yi - ye___ Ta a - vɔ na le - gba yi - ye___ Ta - ma-kloe

ho - tsui - tɔ ne ta a - vɔ na le - gba le - gba le a - vi dzi be a - vɔ la me - su yeo, yi - ye___

In the second example, which is slightly more complex, there are three shifts. The song starts by using B, A, and G as a trichord, followed by the use of the trichords A, G, and F, and then D, C, and B♭.

Example XIV–6

A - za yi sɔ - ke - le Ðɔ - nu ge ne shi___ Ðɔ - nu wɔ - ye___ A - za

The fourth type of melodic structure is limited to the use of a sequence of major thirds and minor seconds. The pattern could be C–B–G–F–E–C, C–B–G–F#–E–C, or C–B–A–F–E–C (Example XIV–1, D). Only one major second is used in any one of the foregoing patterns, either F–G or A–B; it is therefore the other intervals that characterize the structure. The intervals of fourths and fifths implied in the patterns are also used. Two examples of songs based on this structure follow.

Example XIV–7

Dze - hɔ̃ ɖu - gu - si do ɖa - gbe Ka - dza ɖeâ - go loo_____ Hũa nya ge mie - va.

The fifth structure allows for the use of tetrachords (conjunct sequences of four tones) or pentachords (conjunct sequences of five tones) (Example XIV–1, E). This structure allows the greatest flexibility in the choice of intervals and melodic patterns. However, there is a tendency to limit melodic movement to the frequent use of small intervals—seconds, thirds, and fourths—except where a vocal style makes deliberate use of melodic leaps. The melodies based on this structure may be hexatonic (six tones) (Example XIV–8, a) or heptatonic (seven tones) (Examples XIV–8, b and c).

Example XIV–8

a.   Hehe

Nya - vi - la - mbo___ Nya - vi - la - mbo ku - mbe ka - la - la___ Nya - vi - la - mbo ku - mbe

ka - la - la kwa - ku te - mbe - la - la Nya - mu - se - va___ Nya - mu - se - va ku - mbe

ka - la - la___ Nya - vi - se - va ku - mbe ka - la - la kwa - ku te - mbe - la___

b.   Ewe

Mi - nya wli loo___ Vo - du - sĩwo mi - nya wli__ na Ye - ve vu - tɔ fo vu me-foã a-

dzi - daõ, gbe - ɖee_____ Vo - du - sĩwo mi - nya wli__ na Ye - ve

c.   Mba

O - we nsa - wi - la mwen - ge - le yo - we nsa - wi - la   O - we nsa - wi - la mwen - ge - le yo - we nsa - wi - la

Melodies based on nearly all the structures described above do not always cover the entire range of intervallic possibilities, nor do they always lie within an octave. Melodies can be found that are limited to a trichord, a tetrachord, a pentachord, or a hexachord.

Example XIV–9

Modality

Although the songs of an African society share a common structural framework, they may vary in the emphasis they give to particular tones in certain positions or to particular sequences of intervals. These differences in emphasis are achieved partly through the choice of progressions and partly through the way in which phrases are ordered. A phrase that follows another in a sequence or as an answering phrase bears a certain relationship to the first phrase which is reflected in its choice of note sequences or in its cadence. Hence, each successive phrase is conditioned by what precedes it, and every phrase anticipates the progression of the phrase that follows it. The cadential notes of final and nonfinal phrases similarly reflect these expectations.

Examination of phrases and their endings shows that nearly every note of the scale may occur as an ending in a specific context. Thus, if we examine songs in the pentatonic scale, we shall find that in a number of songs the final tone is C (Example XIV–10), while in others it is D (Example XIV–11), E (Example XIV–12), G (Example XIV–13), or A.

Example XIV–10

Example XIV–11

Example XIV–12

Example XIV–13

Similar variations are found in songs based on the hemitonic pentatonic pattern (see p. 118). The three songs that follow differ in their endings.

Example XIV–14

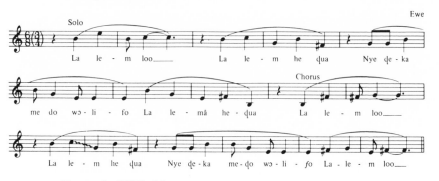

Example XIV–15

Example XIV–16

Other examples of variations of ending tones occur in songs in the heptatonic. Some songs end on C (Example XIV–17), while others end on D (Example XIV–18), E (Example XIV–19), F (Example XIV–20), G (Example XIV–21), or A (Example XIV–22).

Example XIV–17

Example XIV–20

Example XIV–21

Example XIV–22

na mmaa - wa mon - si kyi a - grɔ yi mãã - grɔ yi nsɔ.

It is evident from the foregoing examples that the functional relationship of the notes of a scale can be varied. Just as each note may be used as a final or ending tone, so may each note of the scale be used in specific contexts as a prefinal tone. Hence, every note of the scale can occur as a cadential note of a nonfinal phrase or as a precadential note of a nonfinal phrase.

The implications of this are twofold. First, in a given corpus of songs, sets of songs may share similar endings, similar prefinals, and, consequently, similar melodic progressions. Second, because the function of the constituent notes of songs is variable, there is no single pattern of any given scale, but several patterns. The tones of a tetratonic scale occur in four different forms, with each step of the scale as the *finalis*. The tones of the pentatonic scale similarly occur in five forms, and those of the hexatonic and the heptatonic, in six and seven patterns respectively. For this reason, singers are not as conscious of scales in the form of abstract melodic materials as they are of tonal sequences in melodies, for it is the controlled use of selected interval sequences that forms the basis of melodic structure. This control is maintained in the songs of a particular scale type, irrespective of the patterns in which the notes of the scale are arranged in each of the songs.

The various patterns in which a scale is arranged in songs and which reflect the variable functional interrelations of the tones are often described as *modes* in the literature on African music. The ordering of the functional relationship through particular selections of cadential notes for final and nonfinal phrases is similarly referred to as *modality*. Both of these allow for variations in the character of songs that constitute a single category or musical type. They are aspects of structure which allow for flexibility in melodic organization to suit the vocal range. They contribute to the aesthetic appeal of songs, but have no extra-musical connotations.

Vocal Polyphony

A song may be intended for performance in unison or as a tune to which supporting melodies, melodic phrases, or isolated tones can be added. It may also be made up of interlocking melodic fragments.

Songs conceived of as single lines of music may break here and there into two voices and then return to the basic linear form, when a choice of melodic direction is possible (Example XIV–23). Thus in some forms of pentatonic music, some singers may sing a second, third, or fourth above or a fifth below a note in the main melody and return quickly to the main part, just as in instrumental music some tones may be sounded simultaneously here and there where the style of the music permits this. This kind of organization, however, is essentially linear rather than multilinear, and we may regard the incidence of occasional heterophony as purely decorative.

Example XIV–23

Another variation of this organization is *polarity*, that is, the duplication of melodies in octaves. Some societies emphasize this in their singing when men and women sing together, and others stress it even in separate choruses. Societies employing polarity include the Ngombe, Baya, and Azande of the Central African Republic, the Acholi, Alur, Gwere, Nyoro, Soga, and Ganda of Uganda, the Nyaturu and Chaga of Tanzania, the Luo of Kenya, the Hausa of Nigeria, the Dagomba, Frafra, Mamprusi, and Kusasi of Ghana, and the Wolof of Senegambia, to name just a few.

In addition to polarity, homophonic parallelism in thirds and fourths is used in some African societies. The choice of interval is generally related to the kind of scale pattern on which the music is based. Parallel thirds (Example XIV–24) are characteristic of societies that use a basic heptatonic scale, such as the Akan, Konkomba, and Builsa of Ghana, the Anyi-Baule of Ivory Coast, the Ibo and Ijaw of Nigeria, the Bemba of Zambia, and the Eton and Mvele of the Cameroons.

Example XIV–24

Not all heptatonic traditions employ parallel thirds. The Luo of Kenya and the Nyamwezi of Tanzania use heptatonic scales, but prefer to sing in unison and octaves, and in the case of the Nyamwezi, in chains of fourths or fifths as well:

Example XIV–25

Nyamwezi

In general, the use of parallelism in fourths or fifths is more characteristic of pentatonic traditions. One finds it, for example, in some songs of the Gogo of Tanzania (Example XIV–26) which employ the common anhemitonic pentatonic (see page 118), the songs of the Pangwa and Nyakyusa of Tanzania, and of the Wala and Adangme of Ghana.

Example XIV–26

An occasional third, sixth, or seventh is used in some pentatonic traditions (Example XIV–27), the choice depending on the note of the scale against which a parallel melody is being sung.

Example XIV–27

Parallelism in seconds also appears now and then, though this does not seem to be as widespread as the other types of homophonic parallelism. Sometimes one hears it in only a few phrases of the music. The incidence of this has been noted in the singing style of the Ijesha-Yoruba of Nigeria, who also use sporadic thirds and fifths,[2] and the Nguu of Tanzania.

The essential technique of homophonic polyphony is the vertical relationship between the parts. In some traditions, the possibility of choice of melodic direction in certain positions permits ex-

[2] See Akin Euba, "Multiple Pitch Lines in Yoruba Choral Music," *Journal of the International Folk Music Council*, XIX (1967), 66–71.

tensions of the vertical relations by a further step of a third above
or below, yielding three- or four-part clusters here and there:

Example XIV–28

In addition to homophonic parallelism, polyphony of a more
contrapuntal nature also occurs in some singing styles. The parts
are organized in such a way that each starts at a different point of
entry, but overlaps in certain positions with the other phrases as it
completes the melodic cycle. This style, which can be very complex, is characteristic of the vocal polyphony of the Zulu, Xhosa,
and Swazi of South Africa.[3]

---

[3] For a detailed exposition of this, see David Rycroft, "Nguni Vocal Polyphony," 88–103; for Example XIV–29, see page 102.

Example XIV-29

Furthermore, the parts may be arranged in such a way that an ostinato sung by a group provides a ground part above which the solo and chorus parts are sung; some of the choruses of the Masai are arranged in this manner. They may also be arranged as two overlapping, parallel homophonic melodies, one sung in parts by a group of cantors, and the other in parts by the chorus. This style is used in some of the music of the Giriama of Kenya and the Ekonda of Zaire.[4] Finally, a close polyphonic texture based principally on the hocket technique may be used, as in the music of the Bushmen and the Pygmies,[5] or the concluding section of a Gogo *nindo* piece.[6]

Example XIV–30

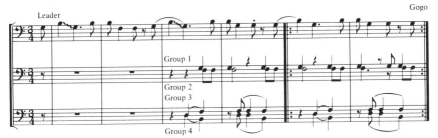

[4] A. P. Merriam, *Ekonda: Tribal Music of the Belgian Congo*, album notes.

[5] For an exposition of this, see Nicholas England, "Bushman Counterpoint."

[6] See J. H. Nketia, "Multi-part Organization in the Music of the Gogo of Tanzania," 79–88.

15 / Rhythmic Structures in Vocal Music

AFRICAN songs embody two types of rhythm: free rhythm or rhythm in strict time. In the former, there is no feeling of a regular basic pulse, no hand clapping or suggestion of a metronomic background. Movements done to such music are based on the performer's subjective choice of pulse, rather than on a pulse derived from the music itself. This form, therefore, is characteristic of songs not intended for the dance proper, that is, for organized movements related to a regular basic pulse inherent in the music itself. Some societies sing in free rhythm for dirges, praise singing, boasting songs, and in some forms of historic and religious chants.

Songs in strict time, on the other hand, are designed over a regular basic pulse. The predominant grouping of the notes usually brings out this underlying pulse, but its presence as an organizing principle may be externalized or articulated by hand clapping or by means of idiophones. The schemes of pulse structure are the same as those found in instrumental music, except that the density referent of the song rhythm is usually based on the fast or fastest pulse, that is, on ♪ or ♫.

Hence, there are songs in duple rhythm—that is, songs whose predominant structure consists of two fast pulses ♫ to the hand clap, the equivalent of four hand claps of two pulses each to the time line. Some songs in duple rhythm emphasize the fast pulse ♪

as the principal density referent, or unit of movement, while others emphasize the fastest pulse ♪ as the density referent. Rhythmic patterns or sections of such patterns based on combinations of the two pulses are widely used.

Example XV–1

In addition to songs in duple rhythm, there are also songs in triple rhythm—that is, three fast pulses ♫ to the hand clap, the equivalent of four claps of three pulses each to the time line.

Example XV–2 [1]

[1] The time line is reflected here by the equivalent of two measures.

Songs based on the hemiola have two components, one in triple (that is, two claps of three pulses each) and the other in duple (that is, three claps of two pulses each).

Example XV–3

Dan - tuo   mu   a - wɔ   oo_____   fi - tuo   mũa - wrɛ - hoõo.   Dan - tuo

mũa - wrɛ - ho   pa - pa.   Ee____   m'a - dan - se   Ku - siA - pea me - nam a - pɔrɔ - bɔ   mũõo

Cross rhythms occur frequently between the scheme of hand clapping and the hemiola grouping of notes of the melodic line. A section of a phrase may be in duple rhythm where the hand clapping has a triple pattern, and the opposite. Hence, either a time line of four steady claps of three pulses each or a time line of six claps of two pulses each is used, both containing the equivalent number of beats, but in different groupings:

Example XV–4

a.

Clap

Akan

Dan - tuo   mu   a - wɔ   oo_____   fi   tuo   mũa - wrɛ - hoõo

b.

Clap

Akan

Dan - tuo   mu   a - wɔ   oo_____   fi - tuo   mũa - wrɛ - hoõo

The organization of the phrases of songs, conceived of in relation to a recurring number of claps or to the fixed span of the time line, appears in three forms.

First, there are songs based on a standard phrase length of four or eight claps (Example XV–5). Where this occurs, the cumulative number of claps will generally be a multiple of four.

Within this framework, the individual phrases may follow the stan-

Example XV–5

dard phrase length, or they may be slightly shortened or augmented with respect to the number of claps. That is, instead of four phrases of four claps each, one may have four phrases organized as follows:

> Phrase one: four claps
> Phrase two: three claps
> Phrase three: five claps
> Phrase four: four claps

Similarly, the length of the sections within the phrases may be varied. Instead of sections of two or four claps each, one may have 2 + 2 or 3 + 1 for a section of four claps, or 4 + 4, 5 + 3, or 6 + 2, etc., for a section of eight claps:

Example XV–6

In the second type of phrase grouping, the standard phrase length consists of six regular claps. Therefore, in terms of its duration, it is longer than the standard phrase length of four claps, and shorter than the phrase length of eight claps. The sections are similarly designed as two sections of three claps. Songs based on this organization may be in duple or triple rhythm: each of the six claps may cover two pulses (Example XV–7) or three pulses (Example XV–8).

Example XV–7

In the third type of phrase organization, the standard phrase length covers six claps, and therefore has the same length as the phrase described above. The main difference between the two lies

Example XV–8

in the arrangement of the sections within the phrase. Here, instead of two groups of three claps each, we generally have three groups of two claps each.

Example XV–9

The organization of phrases within the framework of six claps can be achieved in a subtle manner, so as to produce cross accents between the time line and the melody.

Example XV-10

Changes from phrase lengths of four claps to those of three claps may be made in the same song, giving the impression of changing meters:

Example XV-11

It remains to point out that in all these forms of organization the internal grouping of notes may coincide with the duration of the claps, or they may fall outside the claps. Similarly, the beginning of a song may coincide with the first, second, third, or fourth clap, or, in the case of six-clap phrases, also on the fifth or sixth; or the song may begin between claps. As in instrumental music, both divisive and additive rhythm patterns are used.

SECTION FOUR / *Music and Related Arts*

ETHNIC GROUP MAP OF AFRICA
(SOUTH OF THE SAHARA)

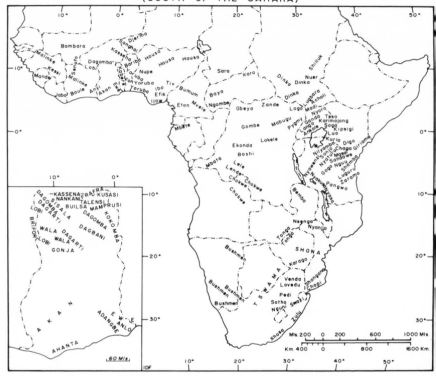

16 / Speech and Melody

ALTHOUGH the formal organization of vocal and instrumental sounds is guided principally by musical considerations, details of structure are influenced by extrinsic factors as well. Form may be influenced not only by the roles assumed by various members of a performing group or by the context of a performance, but also by the nature of the movements and expressions with which music is integrated.

The most far-reaching influence is exerted by the verbal texts to which songs are set. African traditions deliberately treat songs as though they were speech utterances. There are societies in which solo poetic recitations, both spoken and sung, have become social institutions.[1] Instances of choral recitations have been noted, as well as the use of heightened speech in musical contexts. The Yoruba, for example, exploit the overlapping elements of speech and music in their four major chants: the *rara*, *iwe*, *ifa*, and *ijala*.[2] Furthermore, the possibility of enhancing musical expression

[1] For examples of such recitations performed on formal occasions, see the *Oxford Library of African Literature* series, particularly I. Schapera, *Praise-Poems of Tswana Chiefs* (London, 1965); T. Cope, *Izibongo: Zulu Praise-Poems* (Oxford, 1968); H. F. Morris, *The Poetic Recitations of the Bahima of Ankole* (Oxford, 1964); B. W. Andrejewski and I. M. Lewis, *Somali Poetry* (Oxford, 1964); A. Coupez and T. Kamanzi, *Littérature de Cour au Rwanda* (Oxford, 1970); and D. P. Kunene, *Heroic Poetry of the Basotho* (London, 1971).

[2] See A. O. Vidal, *Oriki: Praise Chants of the Yoruba*.

through the choice and usage of the prosodic features of speech is not ignored. The use of rapid delivery of texts, explosive sounds or special interjections, vocal grunts, and even the whisper is not uncommon.

Performances in which speaking and singing are integrated are also quite prevalent. Speech and song may alternate within the same piece: a song may begin with a spoken call-and-response section, followed by a section in which the singing voice is used; similarly, a song may begin with a sung section, followed by a spoken section and another sung section. The integration of speech and song occurs in other ways as well. Among the Yoruba, for example, hunters' descriptions of episodes from their experience in the forest or recitation of poetry about nature or objects of nature may evolve into song.

In many societies, there are conventions that govern combinations of speech and song in story telling. Generally, the stories are told on moonlit nights and on special occasions, by both children and adults. The most important person in story telling is, of course, the narrator, but he needs the close collaboration of his audience, and sometimes of individuals who are gifted in singing, drumming, dancing, or acting. A narrator may change from speech to song and back again, according to the requirement of the story. If a character in the story sings, the narrator must sing, for this is part of the story; if a character wails, the narrator must sing the dirge. His audience may interrupt him here and there with song interludes, for now and then a song may suggest itself to a member of the audience because of the action of the story, the plot, the theme, or the character mentioned. It is not absolutely necessary, however, that the song interludes be related thematically to the story, for their purpose is primarily to provide diversion, relief from boredom, or a basis for active participation by all those present.

As may be expected, the integration of music and language in the different contexts mentioned above not only affects the mode of performance, but also contributes to the distinctive features of a singing style. For example, speakers of a language with a high incidence of nasality due to the presence of nasal vowels and a high percentage of nasal consonants, of a language with pronounced glottalization which is allowed free rein in singing, or of a language with marked consonantal features such as clicks cannot but reveal such characteristics in their vocal music.

In addition to the distinct coloration that language gives to singing styles, there are also linguistic features that govern or influence the formal aspects of songs. These include both phonological and grammatical or syntactic features.

Verbal Phrases and Musical Phrases

The internal divisions that mark off the musical phrases within a song tend to correspond closely to grammatical units of structure. That is, a musical phrase may be conterminus with a sentence, a clause, a phrase, or even a word that functions as a complete utterance.

Such grammatical units of structure do not have to be of the same length; however, where a song is in strict rhythm, a number of adjustments are made in the length of the verbal units to achieve symmetry and balance. For example, where the verbal text of a musical phrase is shorter than the basic time span, it may be followed by a phrase which makes up for this. It may also be extended by means of a nonsense syllable or number of such syllables, or a vowel which can be prolonged to the required duration. Alternatively, it can be preceded or followed by a rest which makes up the required length. Conversely, where a verbal text is longer than the basic time span, the preceding unit or the next one must be proportionately reduced to achieve balance.

Whether in free rhythm or in strict time, coherence is achieved through the use of a number of prosodic links. For example, two units in juxtaposition may have identical lexical beginnings, identical words in final position, or the final word or word group of one identical to the initial word or word group of the other:

A. Identical beginning of one or more words

Memfa Adɔnten nkɔma hwan nie?
Memfa Adɔnten nkɔma Gyamera Siaw.
To whom shall I give charge over the vanguard?
I shall give charge over the vanguard to Gyamera Siaw.

B. Identical ending of one or more words

Deɛ ɔdi kan se: manhyia Aduonimpem awira.
Deɛ ɔdi mfinimfini se: manhyia Aduonimpem awira.
Says the first man: I did not meet Aduonimpem.
Says the man in the middle: I did not meet Aduonimpem.

C. Repetition of a word in end position in the initial or included (medial) position of a succeeding unit

Nana yare a, mfa no nkɔma ɔkɔmfoɔ,
Na ɔkɔmfoɔ na ɔbɛwiawia no.
When grandfather is ill, do not send him to the priest,
For the priest is the one who will steal him.[3]

In addition to the reuse of isolated phrases, as illustrated above, repetitions of whole units or groups of units may be used. Such repetitions may serve to emphasize the singer's point, or give him time to think of something new to say.

When whole units are repeated, substitutions of individual words within such units may be made in the repeats. A name may be substituted for one in the previous unit, or other words may be changed according to the inclinations of the performer or the requirement of the situation. Exploiting this technique of substitution, one can use existing songs in a fresh way to thank benefactors, give warning, cast insinuations, and blame or praise where it is due.

Speech Rhythm

Not only are grammatical units observed in the structure of phrases, but phonological characteristics of speech—namely, rhythm and speech melody or intonation—correspond to analogous features of songs as well.

In general, the relative durational values of the syllables of words are reflected in the rhythm of songs. In the Akan language, for example, there are two basic syllables: long ($\quad$) and short ($\quad$). These are found in both monosyllabic as well as disyllabic and

[3] See J. H. Nketia, *Funeral Dirges of the Akan People*, 77–82, or "The linguistic aspect of style," *Current Trends in Linguistics*, VII (1971), 737–47.

polysyllabic words. Generally, a short syllable (♪) consists of a consonant and a vowel (CV), a vowel (V), or a syllabic nasal (N). A long syllable (♩) may consist of a consonant plus a long vowel or two different vowels (CVV). It may also consist of a consonant, a vowel, and a nasal consonant (CVN).

Modifications of these two basic durational values often mark junctures in speech. In connected speech, for example, final and initial vowels often coalesce, giving rise to CVV structures. At such junctures, the CV is generally given a shorter duration (♪) than it would have in other circumstances, while the V takes on a slightly longer duration (♩) than a CV to make up for the two *morae* [4] that both units cover. The internal junctures of CV–rV in words like *firi* (emerge), *poro* (shake out), and *foro* (climb) are treated in a similar manner, and this is also reflected in singing. Hence, what is heard in singing as ♪♩ for CVV instead of ♫ or ♩ is a reflection of this speech phenomenon.

The durational values corresponding to the two basic syllable types (short and long) provide a basis for the organization of different rhythmic patterns made up of sequences of ♪ and ♩ or their combinations, as well as combinations of ♪ and ♪, as in the examples below.

Example XVI–1

a. CV + CV + CV

♪ ♪ ♪
Fa si hɔ
(Put it down.)

b. CV + CV + CV + CV + CV + CV

♪ ♪ ♪ ♪ ♪ ♪.
Fa kɔ- ma ne wu- ra
(Take it to the owner.)

c. CV + CVN + CVN + CV

♪ ♩ ♩ ♪
Ma men- san nkɔ
(Let me go back.)

d. CVV + CVV + CVN + CVV

♩ ♩ ♩ ♩
Mmoa-tia san- kuo
(The little man's guitar.)

e. CVN + CV + CV + CVV

♩ ♪ ♪ ♩
San fa kɔ fie
(Take it back home.)

f. CVN + CVV + CVV + CV + CV

♩ ♩ ♫. ♪ ♪
Dan -tuo mu a-wɔ yi
(Cold is the empty room.)

[4] A *mora* is the measurement of durational value of a short syllable.

Generally, there is no restriction on either the order or the sequence of words of different syllable types; lexical units may follow each other freely as they do in speech. In other words, they need not be organized on the basis of a uniform metrical scheme based on quantity.

The effect of this lack of a uniform meter will be noticed at the boundaries of the regular divisions of the time span. Such regular divisions may be ignored where the normal duration of a syllable extends beyond it. In other words, what appears in songs as additive rhythm may in fact be a speech phenomenon. The rhythmic patterns may be determined by speech rhythm and not shaped entirely by purely musical considerations.

In a language such as Akan, in which stress is relatively less important than tone, the placement of long and short syllables in relation to the regulative beat is guided by the patterns that a singer wishes to build. Hence, both short and long syllables may occur in stressed positions. Indeed, the same text may be treated in different ways, according to the rhythmic effect desired, e.g.,

Example XVI–2

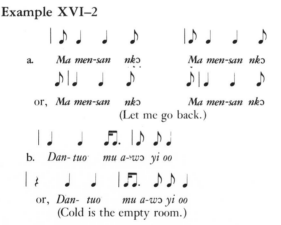

Where word stress is an important feature of speech rhythm, a strongly stressed syllable occuring at the beginning of an utterance would be placed in a position where it would also carry a relatively strong stress in the music. However, succeeding stressed syllables

are not always treated consistently in this manner. The normal speech rhythm would be followed even where this results in the placement of stressed syllables athwart the basic beats of the melody. Hence, irregular stress placement in songs may be a speech phenomenon, rather than something arising out of purely musical considerations.

In songs in strict time, this freedom of rhythmic organization is counterbalanced by the regularity of beats felt subjectively, which may be externalized by means of hand clapping. Moreover, the absence of a single metrical scheme in the text is compensated for in the song by the use of a fixed time span or time line.

The distinction between long and short syllables is not maintained to the same extent in songs based on duple rhythm (songs with a pulse structure of two, four, eight, or sixteen units to a time span) as we find in those based on triple rhythms (songs with a pulse structure of three, six, twelve, or twenty-four units to the time span). The following modifications in syllable duration are used for the sake of rhythmic variety:

A. Instead of ♪ and ♩ for short and long syllables, one durational value may be used for both of them, where the desired rhythm pattern is ♫ or ♫♫.

B. Sequences of long and short syllables may also be treated as ♫♫. or ♪♪ ♪♪ in sections of phrases where contrast is desired.

C. Similarly, three short syllables may be treated as a triplet, if they are followed by a long syllable; that is, as ♫♪ ♩

D. Sequences of long syllables or sequences of two long and one short syllable may be treated as ♫♩ or as a triplet: ♪♪♩

Furthermore, in some African traditions (such as those of the Akan, Ga, and Ewe), sixteenth notes may occur as subdivisions of the pulse where a long syllable (CVV or CVN) is a composite of two morae. The following patterns, therefore, occur in songs based on this pulse structure: (a) ♫ ♫ (b) ♫♩ (c) ♫ ♩. In the singing style of other societies, such as the Ijaw of Nigeria, on the other hand, groups of sixteenth notes representing sequences of short syllables rather than subdivisions of long syllables are not uncommon.

Example XVI–3

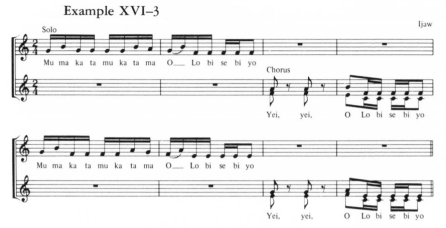

Intonation and Melodic Contour

Another important area in which speech factors are taken into account is that of melodic organization. Whatever the scale, attention is paid as far as possible to the intonation of the text. This is because distortion of the intonation of phrases or the tones of words might create problems for the listener, for many African languages are "tone languages," that is, languages in which tone is phonemic, or serves to distinguish words in much the same way as do vowels and consonants. The following pairs of words, for example, have the same vowels and consonants, and would be homonymous but for the difference in their tones.

ɔbɔfoɔ	[– – – ⁻]	hunter
ɔbɔfoɔ	[_ ⁻ – –]	messenger
bogya	[_ ⁻]	firefly
bogya	[⁻ –]	kinsman
dadeɛ	[_ ⁻ ⁻]	iron
dadeɛ	[⁻ – –]	name of a large tree

Tones that function in this manner are described by some linguists as semantic tones. In addition to these, one would also find tones that perform grammatical function: for example, the difference between positive and negative in the following pairs of Twi sentences is indicated to the listener by the tone. In the first pair, the tones are high-level, and the statement is positive; in the second, however, the tones are low–high, and the statement is interpreted as negative.

ɔnkɔ	[⁻⁻]	Let him go; or, he should go.
ɔnkɔ	[_⁻]	He does not go; or, he should not go.
ɔntase	[⁻⁻⁻]	Let him pick it up.
ɔntase	[_ _⁻]	He does not pick it up; or, he should not pick it up.

Similarly, the difference between a statement and question may also be indicated by tone. In Twi, a question is indicated by the use of a falling tone on the last syllable, as in the examples below:

ɔwɔ hɔ	[_ _⁻]	He is there.
ɔwɔ hɔ?	[_ _\]	Is he there?
ɔbɛba	[_⁻⁻]	He will come.
ɔbɛba?	[_⁻\]	Will he come?
ɔnkɔ	[_⁻]	He does not go.
ɔnkɔ?	[_\]	Does he not go?

The syntactical relationship between words may also be marked by tone. In Twi, for example, the relationship between a noun and its qualifying adjective of quality may be expressed by intonation. Thus the words *onipa* (man) and *adwuma* (work) have high pitches on the last two syllables but they are pronounced with low-pitched tones when followed by words like *pa* (good) and *tenten* (tall):

onipa	[_⁻⁻]	man
onipa pa	[_ _ _⁻]	good man
onipa tenten	[_ _ _⁻⁻]	tall man
adwuma	[_⁻⁻]	work
adwuma pa	[_ _ _⁻]	good work

Another example of syntactical tone is found in nominal groups expressing genitive relationship. The words *sika* (money), *kɛtɛ*(mat), and *kosua* (egg) begin with a low tone, but change to high when in genitive relationship with a possessive noun:

sika	[_ ‾]	money
Kofi sika	[_ ‾ ‾ ‾]	Kofi's money
kɛtɛ	[_ ‾]	mat
Kofi kɛtɛ	[_ ‾ ‾ ‾]	Kofi's mat
kosua	[_ _ ‾]	egg
Kofi kosua	[_ ‾ ‾ _ ‾]	Kofi's egg

The effect of these usages is to limit the range of tone changes by making such changes a function of lexical, grammatical, and syntactical usages; hence, the intonation of individual words, phrases, and sentences tend to be fixed.

When texts in tone languages are sung, the tones used normally in speech are reflected in the contour of the melody. Thus, melodic progression within a phrase is determined partly by intonation contour, and partly by musical considerations. Sequences of repeated tones and the use of rising and falling intervals or of flexures (fall–rise and rise–fall patterns) in melodies may reflect the intonation patterns used in speech.

On the other hand, the actual sizes of the intervals used in the song and the direction of the melody may be determined by musical considerations. Thus a rising interval may be a second, a third, fourth, or a fifth, depending on its position in the phrase and the direction of the melody. Similarly, the treatment of sequences of the same interval may be guided not only by speech factors, but also by musical considerations. For example, a sequence of high–low tones may be treated as an interlocking series, closer to the actual intonation contour found in normal speech, or as a sequence in pendular movement, a stylized form of the intonation.

Example XVI–4

Slight modifications in the tones of words or word groups are made here and there, especially where such modifications do not lead to ambiguity. Thus a speech pattern made up of low–high–high [_ ⁻ ⁻] tones may be modified to low–mid–high [_ – ⁻] or high–mid–level [⁻ – –]. Such modifications form part of the stylization of intonation that creative performers allow themselves and that become established as melodic usages.

Modifications generally take place where a creative performer chooses a melodic direction that necessitates such changes. However, where tones that do not fall within the desired direction can be treated as auxilliary notes, they are not modified. For example, the sequence E–D–C–B may be realized in the forms below:

Example XVI–5

From the foregoing examples of correlation between speech and melody, it will be evident that the structure of songs must be viewed not only in terms of musical form, but also in terms of the linguistic structure of their texts. While musical factors shape the basic design of songs, the details of internal structure are conditioned by the texts to which melodies are set.

The recognition of analogous features of speech and music is, of course, not peculiar to African traditions. Non-African societies that speak tone languages also recognize this, while others whose languages have marked features of stress or quantity or peculiar features of speech melody take cognizance of these in the details of song structure.

Zoltán Kodály, the eminent Hungarian composer, had some very interesting observations to make in this regard, with particular reference to his own language. He believed that the best types of Hungarian vocal music are those that are not "contrary to the natural melody trend of the Hungarian language." Hence, as Hungarian differs "both in stress and natural intonation" from many European languages, "it follows that music composed to Hungarian words, provided it conforms to the natural pitch of the language, almost defies transposition into European languages." In the same vein, he contends that "the cult of iambic metre" should be broken, because "as natural as iambic verse is to English and to some extent even to German, French and Italian, so diametrically opposed is it to the character of the Hungarian language." [5]

Traditional African musicians do not consider the mold that language provides for song structure limiting. On the contrary: they use it because it facilitates song making and makes it easy to extemporize where the situation demands it.

African societies are so conscious of the relationship between music and language that they extend its use to instrumental forms. Meaningful language texts or nonsense syllables are used as verbal "scores" of mucial rhythms, or as mnemonics for teaching and memorizing drum rhythms. As indicated earlier (see pp. 119–121), there are instrumental pieces that are based on some kind of textual framework, as well as others that originate as songs. The linguistic factors that operate in vocal music, therefore, apply to some extent to text-bound instrumental music as well. Indeed, it is not unreasonable to assume that irregular stress placement and additive rhythms exploited in instrumental music are derived from the treatment of speech rhythms in vocal music.

[5] Zoltán Kodály, "Confession," *New Hungarian Quarterly*, III/8 (1962), 7.

17 / The Role of Song Texts

THE treatment of the song as a form of speech utterance arises not only from stylistic considerations or from consciousness of the analogous features of speech and music; it is also inspired by the importance of the song as an avenue of verbal communication, a medium for creative verbal expressions which can reflect both personal and social experiences. Accordingly, the themes of songs tend to center around events and matters of common interest and concern to the members of a community or the social groups within it. They may deal with everyday life or with the traditions, beliefs, and customs of the society. This is true not only of serious songs of the court and songs associated with ceremonies and rites, but even of simple tunes, like cradle songs sung to children who may not have mastered their mother tongue enough to appreciate the meaning of the texts.

Cradle Songs

If we take the cradle songs of the Akan, Ga, and Ewe of Ghana, for instance, we shall find that the references in them are those typical of situations in the life of a rural community. One must visualize a small town or village in the plain or forest country, with an expanse of arable land lying around it for cultivating foods like yam, cassava, maize, bananas, oranges, and pineapples.

Social life in the village generally takes place in the open. The inhabitants meet to enjoy music and dancing in the village square. Coconut trees, orange trees, or shade trees provide convenient meeting grounds, particularly for the men of the village who like to sit together and chat upon returning from their farms. That is why in the following cradle song there is a reference to "men under the orange tree," for the father of the child would be among them chatting, while his offspring cries for company:

> Men under the orange tree.
> Stop crying, child of a prince.
> Stop crying, child of a grandchild.
> It is not yours, grandchild of wealth.
> Stop crying, child of a grandchild.

Constant references are made to this rural setting in other songs. The child is the offspring of farmers who sometimes find it necessary to leave him at home with a nurse—an older sister, a grandmother, or any willing baby sitter—while they go to the farm.

> Where has your mother gone?
> She has gone to fetch firewood.
> What did she leave for you?
> She left some bananas.
> May I have one?
> No! I wont give you any.
> Are you crying? You musn't.
> Are you singing? You mustn't.

In another song, the picture of the child left behind is stated differently: the child is urged to stay at home and enjoy himself. He would not be without company, for there would be fowl running about. So he is told,

> Kofi,[1]
> Stay at home.
> Beat the drum,

[1] First name of a boy born on Friday.

That the fowls may dance.
    Ken-ken-ka.[2]
    Let the fowls dance.
    Ken-ken-ka.
    Let the fowls dance.

In another song, the reference to domestic animals in the company of the child left behind is made with some anxiety, for the absent mother knows that he needs her protection and company.

Whose children have beaten my child?
    Could it have been kids?
Whose children have beaten my child?
    Could it have been lambs?
Whose children have beaten my child?
    Could it have been kittens?

Yet, there are indications in cradle songs that farmers love their work and that the wives of farmers are proud of their lot.

If you are hungry, cook youself a meal.
    Why do you cry?
You are the child of a yam farmer.
    Why do you cry?
You are the child of a cocoyam[3] farmer.
    Why do you cry?

References to food are common in cradle songs, as it is believed by adults to be one of a child's main interests. Thus the child is told,

Stop crying.
There is a piece of yam roasting in the fire for you.
Stop that we may get it ready for you.
Stop that we may get it ready for you.
      *   *   *
How I love to eat cornmeal!
When I squash it and squash it,
I squash it in the dish.
O how I love to eat cornmeal.
      *   *   *

[2] A drum rhythm.
[3] The edible root or stem of any aroid.

Robust, robust! You have had a fill.
You will be strong when I come back.
You will be robust when I come back.

The mood of the child provides another source of referential themes in cradle songs. As one song puts it, there are two contrasting moods:

Kwame Abosiabo,
You cry when you are hungry,
But play when you have eaten.

What all mothers want to see is the happy child, so the little one is frequently told not to cry.

Stop crying, stop crying.
Stop that none may see your throat.
There is a gold nugget in your throat.
Stop crying that none may see your throat.

In other songs, the baby is told not to cry because "Mommy doesn't like it. Daddy doesn't like it," or because his food is almost ready.

To make the child happy, the cradle song does not confine itself to entreaties. It incorporates many play elements, in the form of nonsense syllables or in the form of phrases whose sound sequence or rhythm would amuse him. As the mother sings, she rocks the baby to the rhythm, or handles him in particular ways to make him laugh. Some of the lines inserted into cradle songs give an indication of the way the child will be handled as he is entertained with the song:

Show your face,
Show the back of your head.
          *   *   *
Spread it, spread it.
Spread your baby's sleeping mat.
Spread your baby's tail!

There may also be references to things that adults consider silly or impolite to mention, but that children find amusing to hear:

Where are you going, morning star?
I am going to the kitchen of Komete's mother.
Whatever for?
To eat the guts of fish.
To Komete's mother for waste matter.
To Komete's mother for waste matter.

Cradle songs are not confined to subjects of interest to children. A mother may use them for conveying matters of personal interest, for reflection, or for commentary. Hence, the theme of strained relations, envy, and jealousy also come into cradle songs. Women in polygamous homes, for example, have a habit of referring to their rivals in cradle songs, particularly where their relationship is unhappy, for the child always gives one a good pretext for singing within the hearing of others. Such songs are framed in a way that shows triumph over the envious rival:

Someone would like to have you for her child,
    But you are my own.
Someone wished she had you to nurse you
    on a good mat.
Someone wished you were hers:
    She would put you on camel blanket.
But I have you to rear you on a torn mat.
Someone wished she had you,
    But I have you.

The story is told that the two wives of a certain man were both expecting babies. One of them happened to be the husband's favorite, so he gave her the choicest of everything, and fed her well. The woman is said to have been given meat and salt, symbols of affluence. (In the days when this took place, salt was a very precious commodity.) The other woman, who had nothing of the sort, lived on vegetables from the farm, on the leaves of cocoyam. When the women delivered their babies, the child of the neglected woman was big and strong, while that of her favored rival was weak and lean; so the triumphant mother nursed her baby with the following cradle song, which has become part of the general repertoire:

Child of cocoyam leaves: plump and robust.
Child of cocoyam leaves: plump and robust.
Child of meat and salt is weak and lean.

Whatever may engage the attention of a mother, she never forgets the joy that the child brings to her. So she can sing in contentment,

If you are not beautiful,
I don't mind at all,
For your skin is smooth and healthy,
Quite so!

There are always moments when a mother becomes anxious about her child—moments of sickness or periods of separation from the child. This feeling is expressed in cradle songs such as the following:

Who took away my child?
Is the one who took away my child a woman or a man?
If a woman, she would know what it means to bring forth
    a child.
        Kwakye's child,
        I am anxious and troubled.
        Kwakye's child,
        I am anxious and troubled.

But there are other kinds of anxiety from which she is saved by the customary laws of her society. Thus she can sing confidently,

Little one, come let me feed you.
If you divorce me, you cannot
    take away my child.
Little one, come let me feed you.

(The question of who takes legal custody of her child in the event of separation or divorce does not arise in a matrilineal society, for the child belongs to his mother's lineage.)

Reflective Songs

The foregoing examples represent a simple, straightforward style of song composition based on equally simple themes. But there are also songs that are more complex in their references, songs based on the use of allusions and poetic images conceived in the style of proverbs, or songs which exploit the evocative power of names and by-names. They may be reflective or philosophical, sentimental or satirical, humorous or comic:

That which befits a man—befits him.
But a rope around the neck does not fit a fowl.
Three ears do not fit a head.
Hired trousers and shirt can never fit a man.
Even if the trousers are not too tight around your legs,
The shirt will be too loose around your neck.
* * *
It is the ambition of the star to shine like the moon,
Although God never intended it.
If the fowl had a hoe,
It would have performed great deeds on the dunghill.[4]

Songs such as these may be intended to entertain, inform, praise, insult, exhort, warn, or inspire their audiences, or perform similar functions. Like cradle songs, they may be addressed to individuals, either commoners or kings, dead or alive, personified creatures and objects of nature, or supernatural beings and forces; they may relate to the present or the past. Those that relate to the present may be topical, and may focus on incidents or on individuals who deserve to be praised, criticised, or ridiculed. Those who are praised may be mentioned by name, while the subject of adverse comment may be taunted or exposed through the use of appropriate allusions or oblique references:

He sits under the short palm tree drinking palmwine.
Some day you will see our king.
Some day you will see our king and be envious.[5]
* * *

---

[4] Ulli Beier and Bakare Gbadamosi, *Yoruba Poetry* (Ibadan, 1959), 39–40.
[5] An Akan *mmobomme* song (see p. 25).

It is a hen saying this.
If it had been a cock, I would have replied.
It is a hen saying this.[6]

In the same vein, words of advice or warning and expressions of sympathy or protest may be communicated through songs:

Let the fowl lay its thirty eggs,
And let the hawk take away twenty.
Let the fowl lay its thirty eggs,
And the hawk take them: I am fed up!
The rover of the town is in it,
The male crocodile who owns the nation,
Kwadwo, the shade tree of the grassland,
Let no one stir up Kurunku, lest I get involved:
I don't want trouble.
Cockrel, the time has come to be on your guard,
For people are jealous of Kusi.
   Yes, indeed!
The whole of Wenchi is jealous of Kusi.
   Truly, they are.
   Cockrel,
   Be on your guard.
         *   *   *
Chief Kusi is in trouble:
Who is free from troubles?
Gyan that loves none,
Who can say that he is free from troubles?
Gyan that loves none,
Let us hasten to rescue him.[7]

Historical Songs

One of the most important categories of songs found in African societies may be described as "songs of the elders." They remind people of the past and of the values of a society, and require some knowledge of oral tradition before one can understand them.

---

[6] D. I. Nwoga, "The Concept and Practice of Satire among the Igbo," *The Conch*, III/2 (1971), 41.

[7] J. H. Nketia, *Folk Songs of Ghana* (Legon, 1963), 177.

They have been described as historical songs in the literature on African music, even though, with a few exceptions, what they generally provide is not detailed narration of events, but brief allusions to significant incidents and genealogies.

The cultivation of historical songs usually finds its highest expression at the courts of chiefs and princes. Here, chronicles of kings and genealogical references that link the present generation of royalty to their ancestors help to strengthen the position of those in authority or to legitimize their claim to power. But such songs are also intended to exhort the king, to encourage him to emulate his predecessors, and to share in their glories and learn from their defeats; they may also be intended as praise songs.

The singing of historical songs may become part of the social or political institution: the dynastic songs of Ruanda [8] and the *mvet* epics (see p. 100) of the Fang of Cameroons [9] and Gabon are treated in this manner. It appears also that the Fon and the Gun of Dahomey have a similar variety of historical song. Gilbert Rouget describes purely historical chants such as those performed by the *kpanligan*, in which a singer "recites the history of the kingdom and sings praises starting with Hwegbadja, who is considered to be the founder of the dynasty of the Kings of Abomey," and also texts like those of the *baye*, which abound in historical references. Other song types embodying historical allusions are those performed by the *hasino* "singers of long songs," and *ajogan* court music performed by the wives of the king under the leadership of an elder, to the accompaniment of drums and bells. [10]

Among the Akan, similar songs are performed by the *kwa-dwomfoɔ* court minstrels. Their songs, addressed to the reigning chief, begin with a verse in which his parentage and succession are established, before the main body of the songs is presented. The concept of the past as a force in the present comes out in the recita-

[8] See A. Kagame, *La Poesie Dynastique au Rwanda* (Brussels, 1951); A. Coupez and M. d'Hertefelt, *La Royaute Sacrée de l'ancien Rwanda* (Tervuren, 1964); and A. Coupez and T. Kamanzi, *Littérature de Cour au Rwanda*.

[9] See Eno Belinga, *Littérature et Musique Populaire en Afrique Noire* (Paris, 1965), 118–24.

[10] G. Rouget, "Court Songs and Traditional History in the Ancient Kingdoms of Porto-Novo and Abomey," in *Essays on Music and History in Africa*, ed. K. P. Wachsmann (Evanston, 1971), 27–69.

tion, which usually takes place on memorial Sundays (*Akwasidae*).[11] The founder of the nation and his great successors are told to wake up:

> Wake up, Adu, descendant of Kɔrɔbea Asante.
> Ɔsɛe Tutu, permit me to call you thus.[12]
> Who would not like to be the child of Owusu Panin of
>   Edweso and Akua Bakoma renowned for gold nug-
>   gets? [13]
> If anyone had it that way, he would welcome it.
> Dɔmmirefa that keeps vigil,
> O child of Atie Difie, wake up.[14]

The rest of the material consists of eulogies and references to exploits of ancestor kings and the names of those defeated or captured in battle. The recitals are sung by two male singers. Breaks in the singing are filled in by talking drums, followed by talking trumpets, all of which play "texts" that relate to the historical chant or praise the reigning monarch.[15]

The historical chants of the Dagomba of Ghana are usually performed by players of the one-string fiddle, or by the leader of the *lunsi* hourglass drummers. They are presented in sections, and each section is rounded off with brief drumming. As in other historical chants, references to incidents and genealogies provide the main thematic material. These are often given in fragments which are repeated or elaborated, for a recital can go on for as long as three hours, depending on the occasion. Every Dagomba ruler is associated with a proverb or a favorite saying by which he is identified. The texts function as titles, and are quoted at appropriate points in historical and praise chants or in recitals of the chronology of chiefs.

---

[11] Every forty-two days, a Sunday is set aside for honoring the memory of ancestor chiefs.

[12] Ɔsɛe Tutu (d. 1721) was the founder of the Ashanti nation.

[13] Owusu Panin and Akua Bakoma were the parents of Prempeh II (1892–1970), during whose reign this text was recorded.

[14] Atie Difie (Manu) was the mother of Ɔsɛe Tutu.

[15] These instruments reproduce the intonation and rhythm of spoken texts. The languages in which this is possible are tone languages, that is, languages in which intonation constitutes as much a part of the formation of words as vowels and consonants. For further information, see J. H. Nketia, "Surrogate Languages of Africa," *Current Trends in Linguistics*, VII (1971), 699–732.

Naa Gbewaa, father of many children,
The first born of Korle Bukali,
He stated that
When a lot of lies are being told,
It is truth that stands.
Abudu, the first born of Yakula,
Was the conqueror of the Basari,
The son of Asibi said that
A person who hates him
Can never resemble God. . . .

There are many occasions for this kind of recital, but the most frequent is the weekly drumming session in the chief's courtyard. On such occasions, one would hear not only praises and accounts of royal genealogies and the reigns of chiefs, but also accounts of royal battles, chanted in song form.

The tradition of historical songs is found among societies of the savannah belt of west Africa—in Senegal, Gambia, Guinea, Mali, and Niger, where the professional singer, the *griot*, makes this and praise singing his specialization.[16] As observers have noted, the musical functions of the *griot* may be politically motivated to a high degree.[17]

General Songs

In addition to songs of a personal, topical, and historical nature, one should take note of those that deal in a general way with philosophical and religious themes, or with specific problems of man's existence in the universe. Included in this group are songs that reflect on the social order in general, as opposed to the conflicts and stresses that it generates. Among the Ibo, for example, the position of *ozo* title holders is affirmed once a year at a special festival. According to R. N. Egudu, this title "endows every full-fledged holder with the highest social status and concomitant rights and privileges. He becomes a member of the aristocracy who rule

[16] See Francis Bebey, *Musique de l'Afrique*, 36.
[17] See Charles H. Cutter, "The Politics of Music in Mali," *African Arts*, I/3 (1968), 38–39, 74–77.

the land and control the judicial system." This title also "insures the holder against insults and indignities both in private and in public." *Ozo* title poems may be connected with a person's achievements, occupation, and experiences, e.g.,

I am:
One who tills hills.
One who with yams challenges soil.
Knife that clears bushes,
Barn that is wide,
Bush that yields wealth,
Bush that is collossal,
Bush that is fearful.

      *   *   *

I am:
Tiger that defends neighbours.
King that is liked by public.
Fame that never wanes.[18]

There are also song texts that relate to man's environment—to the physical environment, as well as to man's encounter with various creatures. The songs of occupational groups such as hunters, fishermen, and pastoralists embody themes based on these. The *ijala* chants of the Yoruba, an example of which is quoted below, are rich in descriptions of animals and other objects of nature.

The buffalo is death
    that makes a child climb a thorn tree.
When the buffalo dies in the forest
    the head of the household is hiding in the roof.
When the hunter meets the buffalo
    he promises never to hunt again.
He will cry out: "I only borrowed the gun!
    I only look after it for my friend!"
Little he cares about your hunting medicines:
    he carries two knives on his head,

[18] R. N. Egudu, "Igodo and Ozo Festival Songs and Poems," *The Conch*, III/2 (1971), 76–88.

Little he cares about your danegun,
  he wears the thickest skin.
He is the butterfly of the savannah:
  he flies along without touching the grass.
When you hear thunder without rain—
  it is the buffalo approaching.[19]

Another important subject which inspires the themes of song texts is that of belief and worship. Here we find not only songs of praise, invocation, and prayer addressed to individual gods, but also songs that deal with other themes relevant to worship or to spiritual and moral values. The repertoire of songs sung during *kple* worship of the Ga of Ghana, for instance, covers a variety of themes which can be grouped into five sections. The first section includes songs about Nyonmo, God the Supreme Being:

Man, lord of earth's life giving force,
  looks up to God.
Earth sustains us,
  but God is supreme.
When the fowl drinks water,
  it looks up and shows it to God.
God is supreme.

This section of the service contains the smallest number of songs, for the Supreme Being is not the main focus of worship, even though he is acknowledged in the songs. It is the pantheon of lesser beings below Nyonmo the Supreme Being who form the primary focus of worship. The second section, which contains the bulk of *kple* songs, refers to these gods individually and sometimes collectively. Their attributes as well as their functions and relationships provide the material for the texts of the songs. Conscious of the place they occupy in their lives, their worshipers proclaim,

Outside the house,
I stand to behold the gods
As they foregather in splendor.
The gods we worship, we fear them,
But they guard us.

[19] Ulli Beier and Bakare Gbadamosi, *Yoruba Poetry*, 36, and Beier, *Yoruba Poetry: An Anthology of Traditional Poems* (Cambridge, 1970), 80.

The third section includes songs that refer to nature symbols and manifestations—songs about various types of fish, a limited number of birds, plants, and the seasons:

> Do not tell the story of Onwe lest he hears it
> The rains of Gbo season do not fill little wells full with
> water.
> Later rains (*onwata*) which do are falling.

The fourth section in the repertoire of *kple* includes a few songs that make particular reference to some of the ritual materials and symbols of worship:

> I mean the bundle of seven little sticks.
> It is crossed as one goes in.
> It is crossed as one comes out,
> The bundle of seven little sticks.

The bundle referred to is fixed at the entrance to the inner compound of the house of a god, or the entrance to the residence of a priest when it is within the sacred compound. It serves as a sign of warning to all those entering the compound, for everybody must enter with bare feet as a mark of reverence. The sticks are also supposed to have the psychological effect of disarming anyone who enters the area with bad intentions, and crossing them provides an asylum to anyone in danger. The last group of songs refers mainly to the affairs of the community of worshipers. These songs deal with interpersonal relationships, and make allusions to historical events and other matters of interest to worshipers.

> It is overdone.
> The matter between Gomua, Efutu and the Ga.
> It has reached the limit.
>
>   *   *   *
>
> They will all come here, all of them
> The valiant cedar and the unflinching silk cotton.
> All that comprises Gomua will fall in my lap.
>
>   *   *   *
>
> When I get something, my relations flock to me.
> When I incur debts, my relations flee from me.[20]

[20] For a detailed exposition of the songs of *kple*, see Marion Kilson, *Kpele Lala, Ga Religious Songs and Symbols* (Cambridge, 1971).

Repertoire of Songs

In building up a repertoire of songs based on the foregoing themes for any given occasion or for performance by any particular social group, African societies appear to be guided by two considerations. First, they take into account the contextual function of the repertoire as a whole. Second, they consider the function of individual items of the repertoire in relation to specific situations and specific purposes, as well as the latitude that the nature of the context allows for social interaction.

Since the repertoire of songs performed by a social group may be intended for recreation, work, war, a ceremony, a rite, or a festival, the mood of the occasion as well as the actual events are naturally reflected in the words of the songs and guide the choice of themes. Thus, one would expect the songs of Ogun festival to include references to Ogun, just as one would expect the songs of warrior organizations to include heroic themes. The repertoire of songs for any given occasion may, however, go beyond this primary requirement. It may include other themes that enable the performers to meet the needs of changing situations or moods, or themes that reflect the concerns of the performers or the values of their society. Thus, all the songs of a rain rite would not necessarily reflect the entire range of themes used in this context. This applies to other categories as well, like fertility songs, circumcision songs, harvest songs, work songs, war songs, etc., for the themes of songs are not rigidly compartmentalized. Contextual categories and thematic categories may overlap. Songs about death, for example, are not confined to dirges or mourning songs. They may be found in other contexts, including even songs performed in recreational contexts. Songs embodying historical allusions may be found not only in the special sphere of court music, but also in the songs of warrior associations, funeral songs, or ceremonial dirges in which lineage histories and genealogies are recounted,[21] or even in children's songs, as in the following example from Vendaland:

[21] See J. H. Nketia, *Funeral Dirges of the Akan People.*

I walked out with a small (earthenware) dish of meat.
With whom shall I eat? With Sese.
From where does Sese come? Vhutwanamba.
There at Mukwai's they fought and then came back.
They came back and what did they eat? They ate white
    ants,
Ants like land covered with gardens.[22]

Expressions of emotions, of love and hate, joy and sadness, or
praise and satire, may run through different contextual categories
of songs.

Songs which draw on the kind of themes discussed above
serve as depositories of information on African societies and their
way of life, as records of their histories, beliefs, and values. In
some African societies, deliberate attempts are made to use songs
for educating the young—at initiation camps, for example [23]—or
for transmitting information. Instances can be found of the formal
use of songs for making announcements or proclamations, expressing gratitude or appreciation to a benefactor, serenading lady
loves, warning, advising, or boasting. Sometimes what cannot be
said in speech can be stated in song: someone who wishes to
complain or cast insinuations may find it more effective to do so in
song than in speech. This is why ethnographers, among others,
record and analyze song texts for data or use them to illustrate
aspects of their analysis and description, for "song texts are a
reflection of the culture of which they are a part." [24] Hence, some
attention is given to songs as "oral documents" by students of African history [25] and philosophy,[26] as well as by students of social
psychology, for as A. P. Merriam points out,

---

[22] John Blacking, *Venda Children's Songs: A Study in Ethnomusicological Analysis*
(Johannesburg, 1967), 123.

[23] See, e.g., Hans Cory, *African Figurines: Their Ceremonial Use in Puberty Rites
in Tanganyika* (London, 1956).

[24] A. P. Merriam, *The Anthropology of Music* (Evanston, 1964), 207.

[25] For a discussion of the value of song texts as historical data, see J. Vansina,
Oral Tradition: A Study in Historical Methodology (London, 1965); E. J. Algoa, "Songs
as Historical Data: Examples from the Niger Delta," *Research Review*, V/1 (1968),
1–16; or G. Rouget, "Court Songs and Traditional History."

[26] See, e.g., J. S. Mbiti, *African Religions and Philosophy* (New York, 1970).

Through the study of song texts it may well be possible to strike quickly through protective mechanisms to arrive at an understanding of the ethos of the culture and to gain some perspective of psychological problems and processes peculiar to it.[27]

However, the functional use of song in social life or its value as source material should not make us overlook the importance of the musical content of songs. It is true, of course, that some songs give equal or greater weight to the words than the music, while others give more attention to the structure and form of the music than the words. Nevertheless, it must be noted that it is the music that often gives some kind of unity or coherence to the songs of a given repertoire, for a fairly uniform style may be used for a body of songs, regardless of the variations in their verbal themes or allusions. While the song texts provide the significant changes in thought, mood, or feeling, it may be the music that defines or expresses the general character of the occasion or the spirit of the performance. Hence, the musical function of a category of songs and consequently its form of expression would be maintained even where the texts contain nonsense syllables, archaic words, or difficult allusions, or where the style of delivery makes comprehension difficult. For this reason, cradle songs are appreciated even by little children who are not old enough to understand what they mean, and those who sing songs borrowed from other cultures whose words they do not understand still enjoy singing them. (Instances of this abound in Ghana among the Ga and the Ewe, who sing the songs of Akan warrior organizations and Akan songs of exhilaration.[28]) We must thus recognize that the basis for the appreciation of a song may be linguistic, musical, or both.

[27] A. P. Merriam, *The Anthropology of Music*, 201.
[28] See J. H. Nketia, *African Music in Ghana* (Evanston, 1962).

18 / Interrelations of Music and Dance

THE conception of a musical piece and the details of its form and content are influenced not only by its linguistic framework or literary intention, but also by the activities with which it is associated. Music performed in contexts that dramatize social relations, beliefs, crises, history, and communal events naturally develop a dramatic orientation and stress the use of those sound materials, texts, and elements of structure that stimulate or provide avenues for motor behavior. Similarly, music that is frequently integrated with dance is bound to emphasize and develop those features that can be articulated in bodily movement, or to relate its form and content to the structural and dramatic requirements of the dance.

Although purely contemplative music, which is not designed for dance or drama, is practiced in African societies in restricted contexts, the cultivation of music that is integrated with dance, or music that stimulates affective motor response, is much more prevalent. For the African, the musical experience is by and large an emotional one: sounds, however beautiful, are meaningless if they do not offer this experience or contribute to the expressive quality of a performance.

Affective response to music may be shown outwardly in verbal or physical behavior. The values of African societies do not inhibit this: on the contrary, it is encouraged, for through it, individuals relate to musical events or performing groups, and interact

The dance as artistic medium: masked dancers from Upper Volta

socially with others in a musical situation. Moreover, motor response intensifies one's enjoyment of music through the feelings of increased involvement and the propulsion that articulating the beat by physical movement generates.

The importance attached to the dance does not lie only in the scope it provides for the release of emotion stimulated by music. The dance can also be used as a social and artistic medium of communication. It can convey thoughts or matters of personal or social importance through the choice of movements, postures, and facial expressions. Through the dance, individuals and social groups can show their reactions to attitudes of hostility or cooperation and friendship held by others towards them. They can offer respect to their superiors, or appreciation and gratitude to well-wishers and benefactors. They can react to the presence of rivals, affirm their status to servants, subjects, and others, or express their beliefs through the choice of appropriate dance vocabulary or symbolic gestures.

When a dancer points the right hand or both hands skyward in an Akan dance, he is saying, "I look to God." When he places his right forefinger lightly against his head, he means, "It is a matter for my head, something I should think seriously about, something that I must solve for myself." If he places his right forefinger below his right eye, he is saying, "I have nothing to say but see how things will go." When he rolls both hands inwards and stretches his right arm simultaneously with the last beats of the music, he means, "If you bind me with cords, I shall break them into pieces." [1]

Of course, one can dance without attempting to convey anything apart from one's personal feeling of exhilaration, restlessness, or even sorrow, with nothing more specific to express. But I have watched people take turns in the dancing ring to insult one another or express happier sentiments; such behavior does not pass without comment after the event.

Because the dance is an avenue of expression, it may be closely related to the themes and purposes of social occasions, though the guiding principle may be complex. Dancing at funerals, for example, does not necessarily express only sorrow or grief; it may also indicate tribute to the dead or group solidarity in the face of crisis. Among the Konkomba of Ghana, it is the duty of young men to dance at the burials of elders of their clan, of related clans, and even of contiguous districts, if they are sent by their leaders, for dancing at burials is a symbol of clan membership as well as an expression of interclan relationship. [2] For similar social reasons, one will find in other societies that, in addition to what is intended specifically for the funeral, other forms of music and dance— including recreational music—may be performed as an homage to the deceased or as a means of identification with the bereaved.

[1] See J. H. Nketia, *Drumming in Akan Communities of Ghana*, 160.
[2] See David Tait, *The Konkomba of Northern Ghana* (London, 1961), 81–90.

Basic Movements

The basic movements used in traditional dances may be either simple or somewhat intricate in conception. The *dea* dance of the Frafra of Ghana, a relatively slow dance compared with other Frafra dances, is made up of simple movements done in columns. Each dancer wears a set of buzzers on the right ankle and holds a sword in his right hand. As the dancers sing, they stamp the ground with the right foot on the strong beat of the music and take a short light step forward on the weak beat with the left foot. The body is tilted slightly to the right as the foot stamps and then swayed to the left for the weak beat. The dancers look straight ahead; they do not dance "towards the earth."

In contrast with this are the basic movements of the dances of the Akan of Ghana. Here we have a complex pattern of basic steps against seemingly independent movements of various parts of the body, which may be combined simultaneously with hand and leg gestures. While the feet are moving regularly in duple beats, the body may be tilting sideways in similar or shorter durational units, with the hands or arms perhaps moving at a different pace.

In some dances, instead of moving the whole trunk in a simple rhythm, only the upper or lower part is accentuated. In the *nyin-dogu* dance of the Dagomba of Ghana, primarily the muscles of the belly are employed, while the Lobi and Anlo-Ewe of Ghana emphasize the upper part of the body. There may be rotation or upward and downward movements of the shoulders, or expansion of the chest, along with certain arm movements and contraction and release of the shoulder blades.

There are also dances such as those of the Kalabari of Nigeria, in which the hips are used in a subtle way, dances with intricate footwork, such as the *seyalo* dance of the Nguu of Tanzania or the *akɔm* dance of the Akan and Ga of Ghana, and dances with exaggerated leg gestures and raised knees, such as the *yongo* dance of the Builsa and the Kassena-Nankani.

Combined with these are striking actions which may be performed at one specific moment or in repeated sequences, and which may characterize particular dances either as part of the basic movements or as mimed elements. Such elements include shaking (typical of dances in which the muscles of the body or of the arms are rippled), stamping, stooping or squatting, leaping, lifting, or tumbling.

The postures that are assumed in these dances are directly related to the way the body is used and moved. Certain movements are more easily executed from a position in which the back is slightly bent with the knees slightly dropped and the arms held loose, than from a rigid erect posture.

Of course, African societies differ in the norms that they choose to follow in their dances. The same set of movement sequences is not used everywhere. There is a tendency to specialize, to stress some movements and progressions more than others. The range of diversity extends even to quality, timing, and flow of movements. Most of the dances of the peoples of northern Ghana for example, are more vigorous and sharper in quality than those of the south. Superficially, they appear to the onlooker to demand a great deal of physical effort, but this is sometimes an illusion created by the quality and speed of the movements. In many areas, there are qualitative differences between male and female dances, even where the basic movements are similar. Male dances may be angular or sharp, while female dances are rounded and flowing.

Departures from the usual forms may be made intentionally where one wants to be comic or to convey a specific impression. But there is a world of difference between the good dancer who uses deliberate distortions in dynamics or differences in elements of movement for a purpose, and the bad dancer who habitually distorts these qualities.

Formal Relationships between Music and Dance

Although the total impact of a piece of music on a dancer influences the expressive quality of his dance, it is generally the rhythmic structure that influences the pattern of his movements. He derives his motor feeling from this rhythmic structure, whose elements he articulates in his basic movements.

The rhythms that govern the choice of movement sequences

or the grouping of such sequences may be organized linearly or multilinearly. Both the regular and irregular occurrences of strong accents in the linear patterns and the cross rhythms of multilinear designs offer a range of dynamic points at which changes in position or changes in the flow or timing of body movements may be effected. In some dances, there is little scope for articulating these dynamic changes in movement. The basic routine may be prescribed, and the team of dancers may simply follow signals from their leader or cues from the leading instrumentalist in changing from one set of movements to another. Here rhythms may serve simply as a propelling factor which might stimulate expression or animate performance. The music may provide a kind of continuum for the dance, as well as the basis for establishing the dancer's motor beat and his tempo of movement. The xylophone dance of the Lobi is a good example of this: it follows a routine, but the music sounds far more complicated than the movements that go with it.

In other dances, rhythm and movement are more closely knit. A series of prearranged movement sequences or figures may each be identified with a distinctive rhythmic pattern so that changes in rhythm are automatically accompanied by changes in dance movements. An example of this is the *agbekɔ* dance of the Anlo-Ewe of Ghana. It consists of a number of dance figures, each of which is introduced by an appropriate rhythmic figure played on the master drum and continued throughout the execution of that figure. Each figure is repeated a number of times without break, and is linked to the next by another set of movements designed to bring the dancers to a fresh starting point for the performance of the next figure. There are also standard bridge passages and signals for indicating what is required. Anyone who takes part in *agbekɔ* dances must be very alert. He must know the music well and be able to respond immediately to signals indicating changes in movement patterns or progressions. For this reason, before a new *agbekɔ* dance team appears for a public performance, the dancers must have rehearsed privately for several months mastering the different figures that have to be executed in response to each set of master drum rhythms.

A similar kind of organization is used in the *sekpele* dances of the Lobi-Dagarti of Nandom in northern Ghana, the *eseni* dance of the Ijaw of Nigeria, and the *atilogwu* dances of eastern Nigeria. In the *sekpele* dances, the music is provided by xylophones and a rhythm section consisting of drums, bells, and iron castanets played by the dancers themselves; but the signals for the dance sequences are given by the largest drum in the rhythm section, which also articulates the rhythmic patterns outlined by the stamping feet of the dancers. This principle guides the use of the gong or bell in the *atilogwu* dance of the Ibo, where the gong echoes or delineates the rhythm of the footwork.[3] In the case of the Ijaw *eseni* dance, the movements are fixed to the rhythmic line of a song rather than the accompanying percussion, and are repeated with every repetition of the song. Many songs are sung at one and the same performance, each with its set of stylized movements which are mastered by the dancers at rehearsals before they perform on a public occasion. At the end of each round of singing, indicated by a whistle, the dancers follow the signals of the principal percus-

[3] For a detailed descriptive analysis of this, see Meki Nzewi, "The Rhythm of Dance in Igbo Music," *The Conch*, III/2 (1971), 104–8.

Dancing *sekpele* to the music of xylophones

sion—the set of pots played by hitting each one across the mouth with a fan. It is customary in some of these team dances for a leader to introduce each figure by executing the basic movements briefly. This convention is used in the *adzobo* dance of the Fon of Dahomey, the *atilogwu* dance of the Ibo, and the *eseni* dance of the Ijaw.

In dances that stress individual expression, on the other hand, the relationship between the music and the dance movements may not be so tightly knit. Scope may be given to improvisation, and each person may work out different elaborations of the basic movements in relation to the rhythmic patterns played by the master drummer or other instrumentalist who provides the basic guide to the dance, or the dancer may devise his elaborations in relation to the resultant of the combined rhythms of the different instruments of an ensemble. A good dancer usually attempts to interpret the rhythms of the music in definite ways.

In Akan dances which are approached in this manner, like *adowa* and *sikyi*, dancers are guided by a number of principles. The first is the recognition and proper articulation of the basic regulative beats of the music. The basic steps of the dance divide the time line, articulated by a bell, into two or multiples of two. When just two divisions are used for a start, the right foot moves forward on the strong beat of the pattern, followed by the left foot on the next beat—that is, the initial beat of the second half of the pattern. Once this division is clearly established, the time line may be subdivided further. The feet may divide the line into four equal steps, or one foot may move in single steps of one beat while the other takes two steps, one to the side and one forward, the side step starting on an unaccented portion of the line and the forward step on the main accent. Further elaboration may be achieved by stepping off the beat, that is, giving the beat to the raised foot rather than to the foot on the ground.

The second principle concerns movements of various parts of the body—the hands and the trunk—which may be coordinated with the steps in relation to the divisions of the time line. It is here that the dynamic accents of the drums, which may coincide or lie athwart the regulative beats of the time line, may be articulated in definite movements of some part of the body. In this connection, tones which emerge prominently from the total complex may be taken into account. In the music of a drum ensemble, they may be the tones of the small drum, the medium-pitched drum, or the master drum. As the master drummer changes his patterns, these accentual points may change, giving the dancer who is following the music an opportunity to vary the rhythm of his body movements. Of course, not every tone need be articulated in movement. If this were done, the dance would become fussy and would lose clarity; in addition, the fluidity of its movements would be distorted.

The third principle governs the speed or timing of movements. Suggestions of rapid movement may be embodied in a pattern, in the values of the durational units, or in the use of a drumroll. The dancer may take short steps, do quick turns, spins, and so forth, according to the character of the music.

The fourth principle pertains to the articulation of staggered rhythms. Irregular patterns or patterns with staggered beats may be introduced into the music, and the dancer may adjust his steps accordingly.

The fifth principle is the matter of phrasing. Because a drummer works in patterns which are clearly demarcated from each other, each pattern may be repeated when established. This enables the dancer to phrase his movements clearly, and to introduce pauses or closing gestures with the legs, the hands, the head, etc. It may suggest change of levels, change in dynamics, and so on.

Thus, a great deal of the dance depends on the variety of ideas offered by the music. When the music consists of only a few basic ideas or phrases which are repeated over and over again, the dancer who is interested in contrasts will have very little to fall back on except his own imagination.

Another aspect of music for the dance which may influence the organization of movement is sectional structure. In songs, there may be a part for a soloist and a part for the chorus. These two parts may be different or identical; that is, the chorus may either repeat what the soloist sings or continue with something different. In some societies, this structure is merely a convenient performance arrangement which does not affect the organization of the dance materially; in others, different sets of movements may be used for each part, particularly where the dancers both sing and dance.

Solo–chorus alternation is also used in some instrumental ensembles, particularly in flute and trumpet music; sometimes the alternation is between instrumental ensembles and voices. In the dances of the Chopi of Mozambique or the Lobi-Dargati of Ghana, there are always moments when dancing is not so vigorous, when the dancers may sing in a chorus with the xylophones. The singing thus provides contrast not only in the music, but also in the dance that goes with it. A similar approach is used when a chorus accompanied by a drum ensemble sings and dances. Signals to stop singing and to begin dancing vigorously may be given by a whistle or a drum. Sometimes similar contrasts are provided by varying the texture of an instrumental ensemble, for example, by alternating the full ensemble with one or two instruments, or by including a "waiting section" in the piece of music where the master drummer can break off for a minute or two, or play "waiting beats."

Design of Music for the Dance

It will be evident from the foregoing discussion that the structural interdependence of music and dance makes strenuous demands on the creative performer. Not only must the style and movement patterns of the dance be clear to the musician providing the dance music, but also such details as tempo, ordering of recurring motor beats, balance of phrases, and functional relations between sections of the music and the dance routine. Moreover, it is important that clear guides to the required movements be provided within the texture of the music itself, so that anyone dancing to it can identify and articulate the basic beats, cues for changes in movement, dramatic pauses, and signals for intensification of movement or for the relaxation of effort.

Another consideration is that of the duration of the dance piece. It is not usual to design the length of the piece so that it corresponds exactly to the required duration of a dance, for a single dance may be performed for a variable length of time. As a rule, therefore, the required duration of the music is obtained through repetitions of the piece (with appropriate variations), or through the use of a cycle of songs which fit the particular dance. A number of contextual factors influence the number of repeats. The duration may be determined not only by the structure of the dance routine, but also by the number of phases or internal subdivisions of the routine that are performed. The choice of these may be determined by the musicians. Much also depends on the mood of the musicians. They may decide to curtail a performance because they are tired or because they feel that enough rounds of a particular dance have been performed. This is particularly so where the tradition allows only one or two people to step into the dancing ring at a time, dance for a few minutes and retire for others to follow. It would be at the discretion of the musicians to determine when to break the sequence and start again. On the other hand, there are traditions in which the decision to stop is taken by the dancer, and not the musicians. In this case, the dancer gives the appropriate signal to the musicians to round off the piece.

Closely related to the question of repetition is the problem of variety and contrast. Some musical traditions provide variety and contrast through the use of cycles of songs that fit a particular dance, or suites of contrasting pieces which allow for variations in the routine or styles of a given dance to be made.

Another element in the design of music for the dance is the need for emotional preparation of the dancer, which may be provided for at the beginning of a performance through the presentation of a preparatory song or a cycle of such songs. Song preludes may be performed in free rhythm, and the singing may be accompanied by one or two instruments rather than a full ensemble. Instead of a vocal introduction, an instrumental prelude may be used. In northwestern Ghana, where xylophones provide music for the dance, the main dance may be preceded by a short prelude on this instrument. Similarly, the Chopi, who form large xylophone orchestras, begin their *ngodo* dances with an orchestral introduction.[4] A combination of both vocal and instrumental introduction may also be used: in the Akan *kete* dance, for example, the preparatory songs may be sung by one or two soloists alternating with a flute ensemble; this alternation of voice and flutes continues until the cantor brings in the chorus. The flutes stop while the drums take over and a dancer moved by the music steps into the ring. Some-

[4] Hugh Tracey, *Chopi Musicians: Their Music, Poetry and Instruments.*

times the preparatory piece for the *kete* dance may be poetry declaimed to the accompaniment of a bell. On special occasions, talking drums and trumpets may take part in the musical preparation for the dance.

Music for the dance thus performs two major functions: it must create the right atmosphere or mood or stimulate and maintain the initial urge for expressive movements; and it must provide the rhythmic basis to be articulated in movement or regulate the scope, quality, speed, and dynamics of movement through its choice of sounds, internal structural changes, or details of design.

Obviously, the aesthetics of music traditionally integrated with dance are bound to be different from that of music not designed primarily with movement in mind. When considering the form, structure, and content of African music, therefore, we must relate these to an aesthetic concept which makes the qualities of sound related to movement its primary focus of attention.

19 / *The Dance Drama*

THE structural relationship between dance and music facilitates their integrated use for dramatic communication. This communication may concern itself with the enactment of episodes from history on ritual and ceremonial occasions or during festivals. It may also be exploited at story telling sessions or during the performance of traditional plays designed for entertainment.

The dramatic use of music and dance finds its highest expression in the dance drama—mimed actions incorporated into the dance or used as extensions of the dance proper. A dance drama may be based on one or many themes, without necessarily having a single coherent story line. Although it usually stands out as a distinctive spectacle, it may also be incorporated into the activities of a ritual or ceremonial occasion.

Two of the most common contexts for dance drama are funeral celebrations of such people as hunters, priests, and chiefs, and public worship on specified days of the ritual calendar, special occasions, or festivals.

Memorial Drama

The celebration of the funerals of distinctive people often incorporates enactments of episodes or dramatizations of their social

218

relations, beliefs, or social values. The funeral celebrations of hunters, for example, incorporate scenes in which the experiences of hunters are mimed with weapons, skulls of animals, horns, etc., as props.

> Dramatic scenes may be presented of hunters on small game expedition or in serious hunting tracking animals, taking quick short steps, slow steps, halting, stooping, squatting, finding the direction of the wind, avoiding the wind, aiming, firing, misfiring, getting into difficulties and extricating themselves.
>
> Boys in training may be seen cooking, taking out honey from trees, squeezing honeycombs, carrying baskets and pretending to have come a long way, miming accidents that happen along the bush tracks, dropping things in baskets on the ground, slipping, falling down, while master hunters pretend to be angry with them, give them a slap in the face or encourage them when they falter. Demonstrations of firelighting with flints are given with some of the improvisations that hunters away in the dense forest are forced to make.[1]

This is what happens in the Akan area of Ghana. A description of a similar hunters' funeral dance drama is given by Jack Goody, who writes:

> When a hunter is dead and the funeral is well under way, some six men under the leadership of the elders of the clan sector go to the house where the last death of a member of that group took place. There in the byre are kept the horns (*kpiin iile*) of the larger and dangerous animals killed by the dead ancestors. These horns are gathered up and borne in slow procession, to the accompaniment of a hunting whistle blown by the leader, the most senior member of the sector to be present at the time. When the procession arrives at the funeral, the points of the horn are thrust into the earth in front of the stand. Other hunters present at once jump up and begin to dance, simulating the stalk of a wild animal, the drawing of the bow, the release of the arrow, and occasionally breaking out in victory hallos. Anyone who wishes to show that he has killed more dangerous animals than the deceased can seize the horns and dance with them holding them above his head.[2]

[1] J. H. Nketia, *Drumming in Akan Communities of Ghana*, 87.
[2] Jack Goody, *Death, Property, and the Ancestors* (London, 1962), 103.

The funeral ceremonies of other societies in northern Ghana contain dramatic elements as well. Special instrumental music may be set aside for them. The Mamprusi associate the flute and drum music of *dzugu* mainly with funerals; the Kassena-Nankani perform the flute and drum music of *nagla* at funerals and *naglagao* at the post-burial mourning, while women singing funeral dirges accompany themselves with four rattles; the Frafra play the *bummaworowa*, a wooden trumpet, only at the funerals of elderly men; the Sisala reserve for funerals the music of *nasera* (*dzenbing*), played by an ensemble consisting of one or two xylophones and a gourd drum. The inclusion of an hourglass-shaped drum, a raft zither, and a metal disc is no longer in vogue, although this was the practice twenty years ago, when the music was studied.[3]

Drama of Worship

Another important context for dance drama is public worship, for which special forms of music which may be accompanied by prescribed bodily movements or dance styles are generally set aside. The Akan possession dance, *akɔm*, for example, consists of a suite of about twelve forms, each with a set dance routine accompanied by a prescribed drum piece and a set of songs. There is an opening dance, in which

> the priest whirls round and round after he has first marked certain spots with powder and delimited both his dancing ring and important positions. As many rounds of this piece are played as the priest desires, while the singers call to God, the creator of the firmament (*Oboonyame*). One of the important gestures the priest has to make in this opening dance is to point his dancing sword to the sky and then downwards towards the earth.
>
> When enough rounds of the music for the opening dance have been played, the drummers begin the next piece, called *adaban*. Instead of using swift turns, the priest moves forward along a circular track while the singers sing songs of invocation.
>
> After the *adaban* the drummers play the music of *abofoɔ*, imitative of the hunters' dance, while the singers praise the

[3] J. H. Nketia, *The Sound Instruments of Ghana*, in preparation.

prowess of the divinity who, like the hunter, hunts down evil and protects his child from evil men and spirits. A similar piece entitled *abɔfotia* is played as a sequel to this, followed by the remaining eight pieces.

When the spirit so moves him, the priest may change the order around by asking for any songs or drum pieces he likes. He never stands still. When he is not dancing, he will walk about, do short runs, dash in and out of the crowd, impersonate various creatures, invite people into the ring by throwing a fly whisk or cowtail switch which he holds in his left hand to them, or shake hands with people along the dancing ring.[4]

A similar form of ritual is found in the *kple* worship of the Ga of Ghana. Drum pieces corresponding to different styles of dancing are performed. Each piece has a number of songs with which it can be combined, but in the actual performance the drummers take their cue to stop from the dancers in the ring, and not from the singers.

Because of the importance of music and dancing in worship and the high standard of performance demanded in the *Yewe* cult of the Ewe, a novitiate spends a long time training for the dance. The dances of several drum pieces such as *husago, adawu, sogba,* and *sowu* are learned, for each drum piece provides a point of emphasis or variation in the basic Ewe movement pattern. In the worship of this cult group, sometimes the regular dance may be preceded by some kind of processional movement.

The dance for one of the pieces, the *wumlɔnye adawu,* in which the long master drum (*atsimewu*) is used, is a suite of three pieces of different tempi and rhythmic figures, each with a distinct bell pattern. When the first piece is being played, the priests display their ritual objects. In the second piece, which follows almost immediately, the priests move faster and the excitement increases. By the time the third piece is played, the priests are ready to be possessed. They therefore perform the dance in a state of ecstasy. All those present prostrate themselves and shout *ho ho ho,* or clap their hands to hail the arrival of the divinities.

In some societies, worship of the gods culminates in special

[4] J. H. Nketia, *Drumming in Akan Communities of Ghana,* 90–102.

festivals spread over a number of days. The *kpledzo* festival of the Ga of Ghana for example, is spread over a period of one week in some of the principal Ga towns. The activities are generally incorporated within some kind of dramatic framework, as can be seen in the opening event of the festival celebrated at Tema,[5] one of the principal centers of *kple* worship described below.

Before the community of worshipers assembles at the sanctuary, it is customary for them to precede the main event with spontaneous musical activities. People go about singing on any subject of their choice: elderly men and women may be heard singing prayers for food and fecundity or for peace and prosperity, while others sing some of the songs of the *kple* stamping dance. Many who live in other parts of Ghana return on this occasion to participate in the yearly celebration. Groups arrive in mammy lorries (covered wagons), frequently dressed in distinctive costumes, singing and making merry. Upon arrival, they arrange themselves according to the towns from which they have come: those from Koforidua, for example, form the Koforidua group, those from Accra the Accra group, etc. They may sing songs making references to their experiences outside their home town; those among them who might have lost relatives during the time of their absence from home may mourn them with suitable dirges. In addition, other singing groups composed of those who have been at home all the time may be formed on the basis of kinship or voluntary associations to which they belong. Membership in a group, however, is not obligatory—one may also see individuals singing and dancing by themselves.

A variety of costumes are displayed on this occasion. Some dress as nurses, priests, or beggars; some dress in sack cloth or a fishing net. Men may dress as women, while some women dress as men. Fancy costumes add to the gaiety of the occasion.

Each group sings its own songs to the accompaniment of an idiophone such as a castanet or bell, or any suitable sound producing object, even a kerosene tin. They move from one end of the town to the other, while some of them dance, skip, jump, or somersault, without regard to what other groups might be doing.

[5] A coastal town about twenty miles east of the city of Accra.

The bustle in the streets comes to a head at about four o'clock in the afternoon, when all the groups meet for a formal act of worship. The senior priest and his group form a procession and take their seats at the open sanctuary. The drummers lead this procession, and are followed by a stool carrier, two men carrying pots containing millet beer, a horn-blower, the medium of the gods, other dignitaries of the cult, and lastly the senior priest of the town. A special ritual drum, the *nyaado*, is played in the procession while the horn-blower plays his instrument in the background in praise of the senior god of the town.

After the members of the priestly band have taken their seats at the sanctuary, the senior priest walks backwards some ten to fifteen yards, pours a libation to the gods, prays, and returns to his seat. He is served with a drink of millet beer, and the members of the priestly band are then served in turn.

Dancing at the sanctuary then begins. The groups come before the drummers one after the other. As each group comes in, their leader starts a song. Drummers of the *kple* ensemble (who are also members of the priestly band) immediately join in, followed by the chorus (the rest of the group), who sing loudly and dance vigorously. After a while, the group is beckoned off, and another group takes their place. Scenes of dancing are presented in quick succession. After each group has had its turn, a libation is again poured, and prayers are said to conclude the ceremony. After this, the drummers may continue to play for as long as they wish for those who like to dance and enjoy themselves.[6]

Social Drama

Social relations may also be dramatized on special occasions by means of the dance drama, except that here communication is effected more through the songs than by the dance. However, the singing is always accompanied by some form of dance movement, such as stamping. The performers may roam about the streets as they perform. Some societies, such as the Ga and the Akan of the

---

[6] J. H. Nketia, *Music of the Gods*, unpublished Ms.

Brong area of Ghana, even sing songs of insult in this manner. According to the traditions of the Brong area, the singing of songs of disparagement forms part of the worship of the god Ntoa, who has ordained that once a year, at a special festival lasting a whole week, his worshipers should get rid of all the ill feeling that they have been harboring during the year in song. It is, therefore, a time for group expression of public opinion in song and dance, a time for open criticism of those in authority, and for insulting individuals who may have misbehaved or offended others. All this must be expressed in a social context through the medium of song, but as a collective expression. Any individual who has something to say must do so within a performing group by taking the solo lead or by getting the group to take up what he wants to express. If anyone who feels offended by a singing group wishes to retaliate, he must do so in song with another performing group. Hence, the expression of group solidarity is also part of this institution, and insult may give way to praise and the expression of group sentiments.

In one of the principal towns in which this event takes place, there are three major groups who perform such collective songs. One group is identified with Asere, the royal clan, and a second with Konton, the ward of the common people; these are the two opposing groups. The third group comes from the Bokoro quarters of the town, and acts as mediator or the peaceful integrating element of society. The program is so arranged that the chief and elders of the town have to be present on the last day of the festival to listen to the final performance by these groups and to hear them say how they feel about them. The rules of the institution stipulate that during the entire period of the celebration of the festival, no one can be taken to court or even questioned after the festival for singing songs of insult against anybody. The concluding performance and the rites that follow mark the end of this period of license; [7] thereafter, anyone who sings insults openly does so at his own risk.

---

[7] For a fuller discussion of this festival (called *apoɔ*) and its music, see J. H. Nketia, *Folk Songs of Ghana*.

Dance Formations

The choice of formations in which dance drama is expressed seems to find varying solutions in different societies. There are free dances in which individuals participate as they wish without much regard to others, or dances in which the participants are not grouped with respect to their roles or the basic patterns. In Ga society, the dance of *obene* performed in Nungua as part of the activities of the annual festival is a free dance, while *kple*, performed at the same festival, is organized for limited participation.

Organized dances may take any one of four different 'forms. One is mass dancing, performed by a large crowd of people who make similar concerted movements, as, for example, in the dance of *obene* performed in the Ga towns of Prampram and Nungua during the festival of *kpledzo*.

Second, there are team dances, performed by selected bands of people who usually dance in some kind of linear, circular, semicircular, or serpentine formation. Examples of such team dances are the *miango* and *atilogwu* dances of Nigeria,[8] or the *golgo* and *agbekɔ* dances of the Frafra and Ewe of Ghana. Linear team dances may be performed in single files or in two or more columns. The *golgo* and *senyagere* dances are team dances done in linear formation. The *agbekɔ* dance is also a team dance done in linear formation, which provides for the introduction of individual solos or short displays by small groups of two to four dancers. Round dances are among the most common team dances found in Africa, while serpentine formations appear to be the least widely used. There is, of course, always room for a *pas seul* or *pas de deux* between the major sections of group dances.

The third kind of arrangement gives scope for dancers to perform in small groups of two, three, or four. They may dance abreast, face each other, or describe different spatial designs. The *kple* dance of the Ga follows these patterns.

[8] See Peggy Harper, "Dance in a Changing Society," *African Arts*, I/1 (1967), 10.

Lastly, there is the dance designed for the individual performer within the range of the established patterns of movement. Many of the dances of the Akan and the Yoruba are of this nature, and allow for the individual interpretation of the basic style of the tradition.

Visual Display

Performances of music and dance within the framework of drama or performances which take place on ceremonial occasions incorporate various types of visual display. Such visual forms may depend on the musical type, the nature of the dance, or the requirement of the dramatic enactment.

In some societies, various musical types require special makeup and body painting. The performers of Ekonda *bobongo* music paint themselves with "geometric design on face and chest," while the principal singers and dancers have "white paint around the eyes as well as on the body," and wear feather headdresses.[9] References to the use of such body paints abound in ethnographic writings. The visual aspects of performances may also be manifested in the choice of costumes—costumes for different occasions or different dances, or costumes by which socio-musical groups are identified. Sometimes this extends to the use of special ornaments, and even hair styles.

Another important vehicle of visual communication is the mask. It may represent a special character—an ancestral spirit, a mythological being, or a god. Sometimes other objects of art, such as specially carved human figures, are brought to a performing arena. Here and there, one finds the visual display extended to the musical instruments: geometric or sculptured figures may be found on drums and other instruments, and special decorations or ornaments may be attached to them. Although the visual aspects of performances are not as dynamic as the aspects of sound and movement, they are nonetheless significant in their own right as meaningful symbols.

[9] A. P. Merriam, *Ekonda: Tribal Music of the Belgian Congo.*

Masked dancers from Guinea

Masked stilt dancers from
Guinea

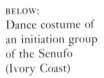

BELOW:
Dance costume of
an initiation group
of the Senufo
(Ivory Coast)

Collaboration between Musicians and Dancers

Close collaboration is always required between musicians and dancers because of the relationship between the structure of the music and the design of the dance, the latitude given for spontaneous variation which demands that both musicians and dancers pay attention to one another, and the need for observing the conventions and modes of interpretation demanded by the particular type of dance drama or its social context. Among the Akan, for example, when a dancer steps into the ring to dance *fɔntɔmfrɔm*, the first thing he does is to pay his respects to the drummers, possibly by giving them a gift. The drummer of the talking drum responds to the dancer's courtesy by drumming his name and praise names and concludes with words of greetings. When this rapport has been established, the drummers will go on playing for as long as the dancer wishes. He, in turn, will be considerate to them by not staying too long in the ring and overtaxing them. The master drummer will watch him and change the rhythms to match changes in his movements. He may anticipate these changes or give him directions or encourage him: "Move outwards, move towards us, take it easy." After the dancer has had enough of dancing, he leaves the ring to another person. As he retires, he may go back to the drummers and shake hands with the player of the talking drums in appreciation.

Since the *fɔntɔmfrɔm* is a court dance, common people who are brave enough to step into the dancing ring must always observe the courtesies that drummers expect of such people, in the way they comport themselves, in the way they wear their clothes, in the reward they give to the drummers. All commoners must dance barefoot, and they must be stripped down so that their shoulders are bare; a dancer who ignores this would be asking for trouble.

In dances of the common people in which performers take turns in the dancing ring, there is similar cooperation between drummers and dancers.

> In the *adowa* dance, for example, various changes in the rhythms played by the master drummer correspond to changes

in the dance routine. A good dancer follows the master drummer, but where there is good will, a master drummer would change the style of the drumming if a dancer changed his movements ahead of the music.

Master drummers, however, get impatient with dancers who ignore the music and may make rude remarks to them. They may play less vigorously or ignore the movements of the dancer.

In other forms of drumming in which any number of people can step into the ring and dance, each in his own way, the extent of collaboration between drummers and dancers is limited and indirect. The drummers may beat their drums louder and introduce rhythmic variations or emphasise particular drumbeats as the dance grows in intensity. But there is generally no fixed correlation between the dance routine and particular points in the music over and above the usual correlation between drum rhythms and bodily movement.[10]

It is important that all those who dance understand the relevant sections of the drum language that drummers may quote while they are in the ring. Society gives drummers the privilege of making rude remarks to those who do not come up to their expectation in performance or social behavior, and may say to them, "You are not playing the game."

The collaboration between musicians and dancers may take other forms. While the dance is in progress, dramatic action may be stimulated and its intensity heightened through the use of instruments which do not form part of the main ensemble, instruments whose sounds symbolize the presence of a divinity, a chief, or some particular character participating in the event, or instruments played merely for creating special effects because of the intensity or penetrating quality of their sounds. A flute player may wander round a circle of dancers, blowing one or two notes on his instrument to urge them on. The trumpet player may play his instrument intermittently to convey a message or create definite effects. Nowadays bugles, whistles, and bells may be used for a similar purpose. Sometimes the text of the songs or the language played by drums and other talking instruments like trumpets and bells

[10] J. H. Nketia, *Drumming in Akan Communities of Ghana.*

may suggest actions which the dancer may incorporate into his movements. Suggestions for particular actions may also be made in the form of prearranged signals.

All these demonstrate that the dance may be regarded not only as an avenue for bodily response to music or a means of communication, but also as a serious art form. That is why an African dancer and choreographer states categorically,

> To us life with its rhythms and cycles is dance and dance is life. The dance is life expressed in dramatic terms. The most important events in the community have special dances to infuse fuller meaning into the significance of these events . . . The dance is to us what the conventional theatre is to other racial groups.[11]

[11] A. M. Opoku, "Thoughts from the School of Music and Drama," *Okyeame,* II/1 (1964), 51.

20 / The Conventions of Musical Practice

ALTHOUGH the prevailing conception of a musical performance is one that integrates music with other arts, it is not imperative that every performance give equal prominence to the sound material, the visual display, and the dance. Some performances emphasize only the music, while others combine music and dance. Similarly, visual displays vary in quality: they may be simple or elaborate, prominent or unobtrusive. Moreover, the nature and scope of the occasion, the presence or absence of an immediate audience, and the nature of the musical message may influence the manner in which performances are presented.

One of the conventional ways of presenting music is to stroll along with it, following routes along which spectators can be attracted, routes that pass through areas occupied by those to whom the performance is directed, or routes prescribed by tradition because of the nature of the performance or the meaning and significance of the music, the dance, or the visual display being performed.

Musical pieces intended to convey special messages or serve as proclamations may be performed in this manner. Songs of exhilaration and incitement, for example, may be sung from one end of a town to the other. When Akan women perform a girl's puberty rites they sing not only in the house of the girl but also in the streets in order to proclaim the event far and wide. Similarly, *egungun* masqueraders of the Yoruba do not confine themselves to one spot. Accompanied by musicians, they parade the town, making appropriate stops as they go along.[1]

Funeral songs intended to serve a similar purpose may be performed by a strolling band. Those who sing funeral dirges in Akan society are expected to move about with their dirges so that they can be heard by those who come to mourn with them. For the same reason, those who sing insult songs move about with their music.

For those who have to beg with music or earn their living through praise singing, strolling around with music is often a necessity. However, unlike other performers who play continuously as they move along, wandering musicians play only when they find audiences. They may play in one spot or move about with their music if their audiences keep moving.

Processions

Organized mass movement such as marches or processions may also be accompanied by music. Such processions may be required by a ceremony or a political event, for the performance of music reinforces the message or the feeling that inspires such events. Processions may also be organized for "showing off" or displaying something of interest to the public. On a ceremonial occasion, a Ghanaian chief and his retinue may parade through the street to the accompaniment of music before settling down in one spot. Among the Akan, this may also be an occasion for displaying the regalia of the chief and the accumulated treasure of art objects of the state.

On important occasions when a warrior group performs its public rites or celebrates its festival, it may exhibit itself by singing and marching or dancing through the streets along prescribed routes. Similarly, in some societies when a new musical club has

---

[1] For descriptions of *egungun* and other Yoruba festivals at which music is performed, see Ulli Beier, *A Year of Sacred Festivals in a Yoruba town*, ed. D. W. Macrow (Lagos, 1959).

been formed and is ready to present itself to the public, it begins its performance with a procession leading to the place chosen for the full performance of its repertoire.[2] Sometimes this is used as a means of attracting the public to a regular performance.

A procession may go at a normal walking pace or a hurried one. It may also be a dancing procession, in which special movements form the basis of the forward progression. There is not always a correlation between the pace of the music and the pace of the procession; indeed, each might move independently, except where the idea of marching or dancing to music inspires the performance. The pace of a procession may be set by the spectators who cluster around the performers and move along with them, or by a member of the performing group itself. During processions which form part of public events, those who assume the role of masters of ceremony may control the pace of movement. A chief may control his procession by halting now and then, but he may also be forced to halt by his masters of ceremony, or by those who recite poetry to him while he moves along in the procession.

Because of the limitations that a moving procession imposes on the instrumentalists' mobility, the choice of music, and the styles of presenting music often receive considerable attention. Some performing groups have musical items set aside for processions; others adjust their regular repertoire by varying the instrumental accompaniment. Some go in a procession with just one or two small drums and leave the rest of the instruments behind; others move to the accompaniment of a few rattles and bells or percussion sticks.

Where particular musical instruments are considered vital for a performance but are somewhat unwieldy, musicians get around the difficulty by providing slings for them so that they become portable. In some societies, heavy drums are carried on the heads of nondrummers, while the drummers stroll behind and play them.

---

[2] For an example of this, see Kobla Ladzekpo, "The Social Mechanics of Good Music: A Description of Dance Clubs among Anlo-Ewe Speaking Peoples of Ghana," *African Music*, V/1 (1971), 6–22.

Performance in situ

By far the most common way of presenting music is to confine the performance to a well-defined but limited area where participants can take fixed positions. There are various formations in which performers may arrange themselves, the choice depending on the conventions of the given society, the requirements of the musical type being presented, and the anticipated forms of social interaction that may take place.[3] In this context, a performing group would generally run through its repertoire of music and dance, or present a selection from it. This selection would generally consist of favorite songs of those who lead the group, new creations, and items that relate to the particular occasion or to current events. They may also simply reflect the memory of the performers, as well as the scope of their knowledge of the music and related expressions.

If the repertoire of a musical type is ordered in terms of the sequences of pieces, this would normally be reflected in the performance. There may be an opening selection, or a number of these from which a choice can be made. There may also be items designed to bring the performance to a close, or a series closely related to prescribed dance sequences. Performances may be presented in the form of a series of events separated by breaks of a few minutes. Each series may consist of a number of pieces played or sung one after the other without any appreciable breaks between them, with each piece repeated a number of times at the discretion of the performers before it is changed. In some cases, however, the number of repeats may be prescribed. The duration of each series depends very much on the dances to which it is related or on the enthusiasm of the performers. There are other modes of presentation in which single items repeated a given number of times are separated by short pauses. Here, each element stands on its own, but the entire performance may go on for as long as required, again with the duration governed by the needs of the occasion or by the stamina of the performers. A performance that starts in the after-

[3] See pages 21–26.

noon can go on for some four or five hours; an evening performance may go on well into the night.

Performances presented on one spot may be given by one group or by a number of groups stationed at different points within the performance arena. Single group performances may be given voluntarily by any socio-musical group; multiple group performances may take place on important social occasions such as funerals arranged by those who can afford to invite several performing bands or the final rites of important people. They may also take place at community festivals, state ceremonies, or durbars (special assemblies of chieftains) at which different groups of royal musicians may be in attendance.

During multiple group performances each group may perform on its own without much regard to the others; however, no one is expected to listen to all of them at once. Spectators or audiences interested in one type of music cluster round the performers. Some listen to the music or watch the dancing for a while and then move on to another group. Only seldom are such performances arranged in an ordered series and presented as single successive events rather than simultaneous events.

Performance Practice

Group performances of any kind require collaborative effort. Collaboration is considerably enhanced when those engaged in this share the same artistic values and are well-disposed towards each other. That is why a basis for group performance is generally implicit in the bonds that join members of a performing group as kinsmen, people sharing common interests and beliefs, or people with similar ascribed roles. These affiliations may be reaffirmed or consolidated during a performance through rousing cries or special calls to alert. Instrumental speech surrogates may be used for the same purpose: clan names or praise poems may be played on drums, or the lead trumpeter of a trumpet ensemble may call the names of members of the ensemble in his introductory solos.

In some societies, masters of ceremony, or "whip holders," are among the officers of recreational choral groups. It is their duty to encourage all members of a chorus to put forth all their efforts, especially when the enthusiasm of the performers begins to wane or when signs of fatigue begin to appear.

The success of performances does not depend only on the effort advanced by the performers. It is also important that each performer know the whole musical piece or the part that he has to play in it, and when to come in and when to stop, since there are no regular conductors to help people out. This is why conventional sectional structures, exemplified in solo–chorus alternations, are greatly exploited, as are multipart structures with different points of entry for the individual voices. The choice of appropriate beginning point, pitch, tempo, or points for introducing other items in a cycle may be made by the person who takes the lead role or begins a musical piece that has staggered entries. On the same basis, beginning and ending signals may be incorporated into a piece of music, as well as signals for changing tempo or changing from one section to another. Where music is closely integrated with dance, appropriate signals are incorporated into the music or into the dance routine. Ritual formulae or set speeches also provide other cues for performers.

Just as there are terms for musical types and categories of songs, so are there terms for basic musical procedures and some of the conventions of musical practice. Some societies have terms for call (*ɔfrɛ*) and response (*nnyesoɔ*), for lead singing (*ntosoɔ*), repetition (*ntimu*), breaking into a song (*ntumu*), and so on (all these are Akan). There are terms for a prelude to singing (*aho* in Akan) or an instrumental prelude, for ostinato (*kumbeno* in Mandinka [Malinke]) and for the transposition system (*miko* in Kiganda), as well as references to style.[4] It may be of interest to note that some of these references are based on the quality of movement or type of performers associated with the styles: thus the Akan, for example, refer to some styles of drumming as masculine (*mmarima mu*) and others as feminine (*mmaa mu*).

In addition to knowledge of the piece and its built-in perform-

---

[4] See David W. Ames and Anthony U. King, *Glossary of Hausa Music and Its Social Context* (Evanston, 1971), 131–51.

ing cues, there is also the question of the latitude that performers can have for creativity—for extemporaneous expressions or improvised variations. Pieces with closely knit structures, such as those based on the hocket technique, leave hardly any room for significant variations. There are restrictive traditions that tend to limit the freedom of performers to make significant changes of their own, such as the court traditions of some societies which demand fidelity to known texts, particularly in historical songs and pieces that legitimize the authority of a reigning chief or his claim to the throne. The latitude for variations as well as for extemporaneous expressions gets wider and wider as one moves from such musical types to those which provide a basis for expressions of social values or social interaction. Songs of insult, songs of contest or boasting songs, songs designed in such a way as to allow for references relevant to the given moment, all give scope for creativity or for limited improvisation.

Solo performances, both instrumental and vocal, naturally have the greatest scope for improvisation. In music designed for group performances, it is usually those who perform solo sections or the parts played by leading instruments who can make significant variations. Limited group improvisation is practiced in some traditions, particularly where performance is based on a given tune which is stated by one instrument and elaborated by the melodic instruments of an ensemble; instrumental ensembles of the Baganda tend to be treated in this manner.

The variations improvised in the contexts mentioned above fall into four types: textual improvisation, melodic or rhythmic elaboration, and alteration in the overall form of a piece.

Because of the frequent use of song texts as a means of stimulating social action, textual improvisation is by far the most common and the most widely exploited. Changes in texts may lead to corresponding alterations in the melodic contour or in the rhythm of a song, where the correlation between speech and melody are closely observed.

Melodic variations may also be made independently where they do not cause violent distortions in the intonation of words that would lead to ambiguities or changes in the meaning of the text. It is possible for a singer to vary the melodic line by simply vacillating between the main melody and its accompanying second part. For example, where a melody based on the heptatonic scale can be accompanied by another sung a third below it, a singer can sing either the main melody, the accompanying melody a third above or below, or alternate between the two, singing a phrase of the main melody and inserting the next phrase into the accompanying melody. Similar melodic variations are also exploited in instrumental music, particularly where phrases or sections of phrases are repeated.

Independent rhythmic variations may also be exploited in instrumental music (and, to a lesser extent, in songs), finding their highest expression in the music of drums and tuned percussion. In drum music, for example, once the essential rhythmic patterns or basic tones which give a piece its identity have been established, other patterns may be improvised by the drummer and linked to them. The basic tones might also be temporarily suppressed and reintroduced, or other configurations based on them may be used. However, all such variations have to be controlled in such a way as to keep the identity of the particular drum piece constantly in view. Any kind of exuberant display that takes the drummer too far away from the identifying rhythms and tones will generally not be attempted by a good musician.

Limited variations in the overall form of given pieces are also attempted. In vocal music, a cantor may start with a simple lead or with an elaborate introduction. He may continue with the normal lead section at subsequent repeats, he may shorten or extend it, or he may interrupt the chorus by singing a lead which takes it back to the beginning of the chorus response. Similar techniques may be employed in instrumental music built on leader–response patterns. The solo instrumentalist also has the freedom to vary the form of his music. The west African xylophonist playing traditional songs may extend them with an introduction, interpolations, waiting beats, ornamental passages, and so on. Similarly, a *cora* player may vary not only the melody and rhythm of phrases and sections of phrases, but may also attempt extended improvisations.

Aesthetic Values

A number of critical problems arise from the foregoing, the most important of which are problems of aesthetic evaluation, authencity, and interpretation.

During a field trip in Ghana, I recorded examples of *kete* drum music and played them back to the drummers and other interested people. They listened intently. The drummers, however, were not satisfied with the first set of recordings, for a variety of reasons: sometimes a particular drum was not prominent enough, sometimes they felt there was a slight variation in the tempo—but these were not serious defects. They had two important criticisms to make. In one piece, the master drum was apparently too persistent; the player should have stopped for a few seconds from time to time or played single waiting beats, so that there would be gaps or appreciable moments of silence while the other drums continued to play. Moreover, while the music was going on, no shouts were interspersed. The performance was not sufficiently animated, so they wanted to record it again. Other comments concerned the style of the performance and accuracy of tradition. One old man said that the performance was not good, because the drummers were "running all the time": i.e., the music was too fast. Another remarked that it was not "the real thing." The performers were all young men who played regularly on state occasions, but there was a particular drummer the old man wanted to hear because he played in the old style. Other critics were quick to point out that there were special *kete* songs, and that I should insist on the complete performance which combined drumming and singing.

Monica Wilson has recorded an interesting comment on a similar problem concerning wailing at funerals among the Nyakyusa. She writes:

> On the plain Selya, they sit packed close together and sway rhythmically as they wail in chorus, following a leader who stands in their midst. . . . In the hills the women who are outside do not bunch together, and the wailing is both less rhythmical and less abandoned. The people of the plains laugh at them for not wailing properly. "In the hills their funerals do not

go well; each one wails separately. Here we listen to one another." "In Selya they lament a death properly; here (in the
hills) they do not; they wail higgeldly-piggeldy; each one on her
own. But we of Selya and the people of MuNgondo and Ma-
soko, we lead the wailing properly." [5]

These comments show that, although traditional music is performed on social occasions, there are norms that must be observed,
expectations that must be fulfilled. The fact that participation in
music on a given occasion is obligatory does not mean that the performance can be done in a slapdash fashion; nor does it mean that
aesthetic considerations have no place in a performance. I have
watched musical instruments change hands in field situations because a player was faltering, and I have noticed time and again the
stern look of a master drummer as he stopped to give someone the
correct rhythmic pattern or urge him to play better.

It is obvious, therefore, that African music practiced and perpetuated by oral tradition nevertheless has its peculiar problems of
interpretation. Although in every generation performers are supposed to play what is passed on to them, each generation may rein-
terpret it, particularly with respect to those fluctuations arising out
of subjective feeling. Some traditions, particularly those of the
court, have mechanisms for controlling change, but this is by no
means the rule.

Another point of contention is the fact that authenticity is relative. Looking back, each generation is likely to find its interpretation more "authentic" than that of the succeeding generation.
However, fidelity to tradition is not the only virtue required of a
performer. I have listened to adverse criticism of performers who
do not move with the times and who insist on playing in the old
style. The comments, however, referred to recreational music,
which is more subject to change and innovation than any other category of music.

[5] Monica Wilson, *Rituals of Kinship Among the Nyakyusa* (London, 1957), 21–22.

21 / Summary

THE indigenous musical traditions of Africa are practiced by societies that in the past functioned as individual political and cultural units, societies that observed their own musical norms and did not have to seek agreement with others on tuning systems or any aspects of musical practice. Accordingly, there are wide divergencies in some areas of musical practice—for example, in the selection and use of pitch systems or in the emphasis that is laid on the use of common musical procedures.

Some of these traditions, such as those of the Bushmen and the Pygmies, those in boundary areas such as the Saharan peoples, or those with a unique history such as the music of the Ethiopian church, stand apart in certain aspects of style because of their peculiar histories or geographical locations. But there are traditions which can be grouped into large clusters, revealing greater affinity to one another than they do to others, and sharing common features in which they differ with other traditions. In other words, the picture that emerges from a comparative study of indigenous musical traditions is not one of mutually exclusive traditions or style clusters, but one of a network of overlapping styles which share common features of structure, basic procedures, and similar contextual relations.

Whatever the specialization of a society may be, an approach to the practice of music as a form of social activity in community life is generally evident. Music may be organized as a concurrent or terminal activity in the variety of settings in which social events take place. It may be performed for the sheer fun of it, for the message that it communicates, or for the outlet that it provides for social interaction or the sharing of community sentiments. It may be a tribute to an individual, an offering to a deity, or a service to a potentate.

The performing groups may be spontaneous or organized, consisting of people either of the same age or sex, or mixed. Other socio-musical groups such as recreational bands, occupational associations, cult groups, or religious associations practice their own music. There are also individual musicians and bands of performers that are attached to establishments—to occupational groups, special households, or royal courts.

There is generally differential participation in musical events. Some performers take on the leading roles, while others participate in choruses or accept secondary roles in instrumental ensembles. The leading roles are usually assumed by people with more-than-average knowledge and command of particular techniques, skills, or repertoire, or by people who are recruited for such roles because they are recognized as musicians or specialists. The instrumental resources at the disposal of such specialists tend to be limited to those in which their communities specialize. The aggregate of musical instruments found throughout Africa, however, is quite large, and includes instruments in all the four major classes. Of these, idiophones are the most widespread and varied, for almost all societies, even those that do not possess drums, use idiophones of some sort, including varieties of rattles, clappers, percussion sticks, wooden slit gongs, bells, and stamping tubes, as well as the *mbira* (*sansa*) and xylophone.

Membranophones similarly have a fairly wide distribution, although there are a few societies who do not have any, as well as others who do not emphasize them as much as it is generally supposed. Membranophones are made in different sizes and shapes and may be single- or double-headed, closed or open. Some of them are used both as musical instruments and as speech surrogates or talking instruments. The aesthetics of African music betrays a distinct bias towards percussion and the use of percussive effects. Accordingly, there is a tendency to include a rhythm section in almost every instrumental ensemble, or to add percussive devices or modifiers to other instruments.

The aerophones found in Africa include trumpets made out of the horns of animals or elephant tusks and trumpets made out of wood or sections of gourd. There are ocarinas as well as flutes, made out of bamboo, reed, the cone of a gourd, or the tip of an animal horn, and flutes carved out of wood. Single-reed pipes are also found in a few places, while some Islamized African societies play double-reed pipes adopted from Arabic culture.

The chordophones played in African societies include varieties of the musical bow, different types of zithers, bowed and plucked lutes, harp lutes, harps, and lyres. Some of these are relatively rare: lyres, for example, are concentrated in eastern Africa, while trough zithers are developed in eastern and central Africa but are seldom found in western Africa.

The scales employed in instrumental melodies are generally based on four-, five-, six-, and seven-step tunings in equidistant or nonequidistant patterns. More complex scales are also found in some societies.

Instrumental melodies are often composed of figures that may be repeated and varied, or text-bound, that is, thought of in terms of song. Other techniques used in instrumental music include the hocket, the ostinato, and the interplay of melodies and supporting ostinato figures.

Rhythm is organized in free meter or in strict time. Some instrumental pieces are conceived of entirely in duple rhythm, while others are in triple rhythm, or in a mixture of both. In the latter case, the durational values tend to be based on the ratio of two to three or four to three. The use of a time line (a recurring rhythmic pattern of fixed duration or time span), which clarifies the regulative beat, is a common feature of rhythmic organization in some African traditions. Rhythmic structures are of linear or multilinear design; in the latter case, both cross rhythms and polyrhythms may be exploited.

In general, the scales used in vocal music are not unlike those employed in instrumental music. However, the actual pitches may not always show a one-to-one correspondence. Moreover, vocal music tends to be greatly influenced by the texts to which melodies are set. As many African languages are tone languages, there is a tendency to follow both the intonation contour of speech in melodies, and the rhythms of speech in song rhythms.

The forms common to vocal music include solo–chorus alternations, solo and chorus refrain, and solo–chorus alternations with ostinato accompaniment. Various kinds of vocal polyphony are also used: some societies sing in parallel thirds, while others sing in parallel fourths, fifths, or octaves. There are instances of parallel seconds here and there, as well as fairly elaborate contrapuntal polyphony.

A great deal of stress is laid on vocal music, for singing provides the greatest scope for participation in group musical activities, as well as an avenue for verbal communication. Accordingly, a wide variety of song types are cultivated, which allow for the use of an equally wide variety of themes. Some of these categories of songs are given greater focus in social life than others: praise singing, for example, is highly institutionalized in some societies.

Musical performances are generally multidimensional in character, for it is customary to integrate music with other arts, with dance and drama, as well as with various forms of visual display, such as masks. There are conventions that guide this integration and other aspects of performance as well. While such conventions ensure continuity of many aspects of musical practice, they do not stifle change or innovation, especially when it appears as a logical extension of established usage.

Moreover, because of the close integration of music and social life, it is inevitable that changes in the way of life of an African society—in its institutions, political organization, and aspects of economic life or religious practice—should lead to corresponding changes in aspects of musical practice or in the organization of performances. Where hunters' associations cease to be active, their music and ceremonies cease to be performed and continue to live only in the memory of those who used to practice it. Where the worship of particular gods ceases, the music associated with them similarly falls out of use. Such breaks in the continuity of tradition do not occur in every locality at the same time; hence, survivals of musical types that were once popular or widely practiced can be found here and there. In addition to internal changes, there are also changes that are brought about by the interaction of African societies with one another, as well as changes that are made in response to acculturation. All these call for adjustments in both musical organization and musical practice.

A number of such adjustments now face traditional music and musicians as they become involved in performances in nontraditional contexts:

—the problem of transfer of function, which calls for adjustments in the conventions of traditional practice with respect to mode, duration, and content of performance;

—the development of new habits of listening, as well as a new basis for appreciation of music performed in new contexts;

—the development of eclecticism, which accommodates the diversity of pitch systems that African music presents;

—the development of new performer–audience relationships based on shared knowledge, shared musical values, and shared critical standards; and

—the development of inter-cultural norms where they did not exist, such as norms of tuning, where performers of different melodic instruments from different areas have to perform in new ensembles of traditional instruments.

All these are problems not only for audiences, but for performers or composers as well. They are recurring issues, which were faced to some extent by the African diaspora, and which now face contemporary Africa because of new values and changing social conditions—changes which are affecting the traditional relationship between elements of music, song texts, selection of musical pieces and musical types, and the social or cultural context, changes which are affecting the body of traditions in terms of which music is practiced and perpetuated. It is those adjustments that are made in contextual relations that will continue to keep the musical traditions of Africa alive; but it is the use of the traditional structures and procedures which define their style and which are consistently applied even to new sound materials that will continue to give to these practices their enduring character.

Appendix One:

Selected Discography

Musical Traditions of Africa

Africa South of the Sahara. Side I, bands 5, 6; side II, bands 5–8; side III, band 9; side IV, band 6.* Folkways FE-4503.

African Music. I/5. Folkways FW-8852.

African Music from the French Colonies (The Columbia World Library of Folk and Primitive Music, Volume II). I/1, 2, 3b–d, 4d. Columbia SL-205.

African Music Society's Choice, Osborn Award. The Best Recordings of 1953, Part I (Music of Africa Series, Number 10). I/3. Decca LF-1224.

African Suite for Strings, by Fela Sowande. Decca LM-4547.

Afrique, Vol. 2: Guinée, Senegal, Dahomey. II/3. Vogue EXTP-1029.

Bantu Music from British East Africa (The Columbia World Library of Folk and Primitive Music, Volume X). II/2. Columbia SL-213 or KL-213.

Bushman and Pygmy Music—Musique Bochiman et Musique Pygmée. Musée de l'Homme LD-9.

Field Recordings of Africa Coast Rhythms: Tribal and Folk Music of West Africa. II/6. Riverside RLP-4001.

Folk Music of Ghana. I/1, 5–7. Folkways FW-8859.

Folk Music of Liberia. II/2. Folkways FE-4465.

Musiques Dahoméennes. I/3. Ocora OCR-17.

---

* Hereinafter, the following formulation will be used: I/2 for Side I, band 2, II/5–7 for Side II, bands 5, 6, and 7, etc.

New Sounds from a New Nation: The Republic of Ghana. Tempo 7007.

Pondo Kakou: Musique de Société secrete: Côte d'Ivoire—Dahomée—Guinée. II/2, 3. Countrepoint MC-20141.

Rhythmes et Chants du Dahomey, No. 1: Sud et Centre Dahomey. II/1. Boite a Musique LD-376.

Something New from Africa. Decca LK-4292.

Sounds of Africa (featuring Miriam Makeba, Spokes Mashiyane, and Leo de Lyon). Fiesta FLP-1358.

Tanganyika Territory (Music of Africa Series, Number 1). I/1. London LB-567.

Tempos Melodies: E. T. Mensah and His Tempos Band. Decca WAL-1022.

Music in Community Life

Anthologie de la Vie Africaine: Moyen-Congo et Gabon. Ducrete-Thompson 320 C126–128.

Bantu Music from British East Africa (The Columbia World Library of Folk and Primitive Music, Volume X). Columbia SL-213 or KL-213.

Folk Music of Ghana. Folkways FW-8859.

Musiques Dahoméennes. Ocora OCR-17.

The Pygmies of the Ituri Forest. Folkways FE-4457.

Musical Instruments

Afrique Noire: Panorama de la Musique Instrumentale. Boite a Musique LD-409A.

IDIOPHONES

Musical Instruments II: Reeds (Mbira) (Music of Africa Series, Number 28). Gallotone GALP-1323.

MEMBRANOPHONES

African Coast Rhythms: Tribal and Folk Music of West Africa. Riverside RLP-4001.

Congo Drums (Music of Africa Series, Number 4). London LB-828.

Drums of East Africa (Music of Africa Series, Number 3). London LB-827.

Music of the World's Peoples. II/2. Folkways FE-4504.

Musical Instruments III: Drums (Music of Africa Series, Number 29). Gallotone GALP-1324.

New Sounds from a New Nation: The Republic of Ghana. II/4. Tempo 7007.

AEROPHONES

African Coast Rhythms: Tribal and Folk Music of West Africa. I/5. Riverside RLP-4001.

African Music Society's Best Music for 1952 (Music of Africa Series, Number 6). II/2. London LB-830.

Afrique Noire: Panorama de la Musique Instrumentale. I/7. Boite a Musique LD-409A.

Anthologie de la Vie Africaine: Moyen-Congo et Gabon. I/9. Ducrete-Thompson 320 C126.

Baoule of the Ivory Coast. I/1–3, 6, 7. Folkways FE-4476.

Côte d'Ivoire: Musique Baoule. I/2, 4, II/4, 6. Ocora SOR-6.

Dahomey: Musique du Roi; Guinée: Musique Malinke. I/4. Contrepoint MC-20146.

Man's Early Musical Instruments. II/9. Folkways FE-4525.

Musique Africaine du Ruanda-Urundi. II/10, 12. Vogue LDM-30087.

Musique du Cameroun: Bakweri, Bamileke, Bamoun, Beti. II/2. Ocora OCR-25.

Musique Kabre du Nord-Togo. II/1, 5. Ocora OCR-16.

Musique Malagache. II/5, 6. Ocora OCR-24.

Musique Toureg et Haoussa de la Region d'Agadez. I/5. Boite a Musique LD-353.

Tanganyika Territory (Music of Africa Series, Number 1). London LB-567.

Voice of the Congo: Music of Belgian Congo and Ruanda-Urundi. I/5. Riverside RLP-4002.

CHORDOPHONES

Musical Instruments II. Reeds (Mbira) (Music of Africa Series, Number 28). Gallotone GALP-1323.

Musical Instruments V. Xylophones (Music of Africa Series, Number 31). Gallotone GALP-1326.

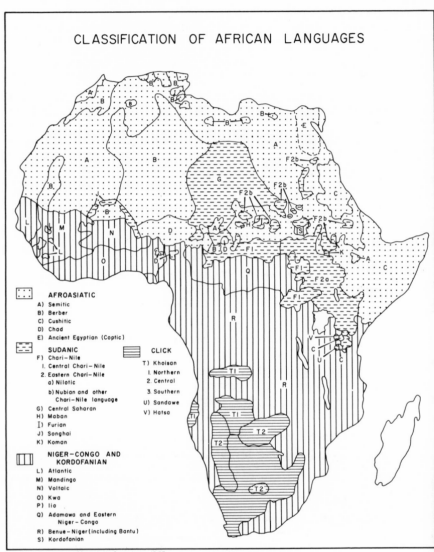

CLASSIFICATION OF AFRICAN LANGUAGES

AFROASIATIC
A) Semitic
B) Berber
C) Cushitic
D) Chad
E) Ancient Egyptian (Coptic)

SUDANIC
F) Chari–Nile
  1. Central Chari–Nile
  2. Eastern Chari–Nile
    a) Nilotic
    b) Nubian and other
       Chari–Nile language
G) Central Saharan
H) Maban
I) Furian
J) Songhai
K) Koman

NIGER–CONGO AND KORDOFANIAN
L) Atlantic
M) Mandingo
N) Voltaic
O) Kwa
P) Iio
Q) Adamawa and Eastern
   Niger–Congo
R) Benue–Niger (including Bantu)
S) Kordofanian

CLICK
T) Khoisan
  1. Northern
  2. Central
  3. Southern
U) Sandawe
V) Hatsa

After J. H. Greenberg, 1963

Appendix Two:

Location of Ethnic Groups Mentioned in the Text

Acholi	*Uganda*	Bondei	*Tanzania*
Adangme	*Ghana*	Brifor	*Ghana*
Ahanta	*Ghana*	Builsa	*Ghana*
Alur	*Uganda*	Bukusu	*Kenya*
Ankole	*Uganda*	Bumum	*Cameroons*
Anlo-Ewe	*Ghana*	Bushmen	*Kalahari Desert*
Anyi	*Ivory Coast*	Bwali	*Tanzania*
Anyi-Baule	*Ivory Coast*	Chaga	*Tanzania*
Ashanti	*Ghana*	Chowke	*Angola*
Azande	*Central African Republic*	Chopi	*Mozambique*
		Dagarti	*Ghana*
Baganda	*Uganda*	Dagomba	*Ghana*
Bahima	*Uganda*	Digo	*Kenya*
Bambara	*Mali*	Dinka	*Sudan*
Bariba	*Dahomey*	Djerma	*Niger*
Barotse	*Zambia*	Efik	*Nigeria*
Bashi	*Zaire*	Ekonda	*Zaire*
Basotho	*Republic of South Africa*	Eton	*Cameroons*
		Ewe	*Ghana*
Baule	*Ivory Coast*	Fang	*Cameroons*
Baya	*Central African Republic*	Fon	*Dahomey*
		Frafra	*Ghana*
Bemba	*Zambia*	Ga	*Ghana*

Ganda	*Uganda*	Luguru	*Tanzania*
Giriama	*Kenya*	Luo	*Kenya*
Gishu	*Uganda*	Mabudu	*Zaire*
Gogo	*Tanzania*	Madi	*Uganda*
Gonja	*Ghana*	Malinke	*Guinea*
Gun	*Dahomey*	Mamprusi	*Ghana*
Gwere	*Uganda*	Mande	*Sierra Leone*
Hausa	*Nigeria*	Masai	*Tanzania*
Hehe	*Tanzania*	Mba	*Tanzania*
Ibo	*Nigeria*	Mbaka	*Gabon*
Ijaw	*Nigeria*	Mvele	*Cameroons*
Ijesha-Yoruba	*Nigeria*	Ngindo	*Tanzania*
Iraku	*Uganda, Tanzania*	Ngombe	*Central African Republic*
Jabo	*Liberia*	Nguni	*Republic of South Africa*
Kabere	*Togo*		
Kala	*Central African Republic*	Nguu	*Tanzania*
		Nilotes	*Uganda*
Karange	*Rhodesia*	Nsenga	*Zambia*
Karimojong	*Uganda*	Nuer	*Sudan*
Kassena-Nankani	*Ghana*	Nupe	*Nigeria*
		Nyakyusa	*Tanzania*
Kiga	*Uganda*	Nyamwezi	*Tanzania*
Kipsigi	*Kenya*	Nyanja	*Rhodesia*
Kissi	*Guinea*	Nyasa	*Tanzania*
Konkomba	*Ghana*	Nyaturu	*Tanzania*
Kontonkoli	*Togo*	Nyiramba	*Tanzania*
Kuria	*Kenya*	Nyisansu	*Tanzania*
Kusasi	*Ghana*	Nyoro	*Uganda*
Kusu	*Kenya*	Pangwa	*Tanzania*
Lango	*Uganda*	Pedi	*Republic of South Africa*
Lele	*Zaire*		
Lobi	*Ghana*	Pende	*Zaire*
Lobi-Dagarti	*Ghana*	Pygmy	*Zaire*
Logo	*Zaire*	Sambaa	*Tanzania*
Lokele	*Zaire*	Sandawe	*Tanzania*
Lovedu	*Transvaal*	Sara	*Chad*
Lugbara	*Uganda*	Senufo	*Ivory Coast*

Shangana-Tsonga	*Republic of South Africa*	Tonga	*Zambia*
Shilluk	*Sudan*	Tswana	*Republic of South Africa*
Shona	*Rhodesia*		
Shona-Karanga	*Rhodesia*	Valley Tonga	*Zambia*
Sisala	*Ghana*	Venda	*Republic of South Africa*
Soga	*Uganda*		
Songhai	*Niger*	Wala	*Ghana*
Sonjo	*Tanzania*	Wolof	*Senegal*
Sukuma	*Tanzania*	Xhosa	*Republic of South Africa*
Swazi	*Republic of South Africa*		
		Yombe	*Zaire*
Tallensi	*Ghana*	Yoruba	*Nigeria*
Teso	*Uganda, Kenya*	Zaramo	*Tanzania*
Tiv	*Nigeria*	Zulu	*Republic of South Africa*

Appendix Three:
African Terms Used in the Text

N.B. The letter ɔ, a diphthong, consists of the *oo* sound (as in "foot") followed by *aw* (as in "saw"). The letter ɛ is sounded as a diphthong made up of *i* (as in "fit") and *e* (as in "red").

Abɔfoɔ: Hunters; also name of the hunters' music and dance, and one of the pieces played by the *kete* drum ensemble.

Abɔfotia: Title of a drum piece played by the *kete* ensemble (literally, short *abɔfoɔ*).

Aburukuwa: A small high-pitched drum used as a talking drum by the Akan of Ghana.

Adaban: A distinctive form of music and dance included in the *akɔm* (possession dance music) of the Akan of Ghana.

Adakam: A recreational musical type performed by the Akan of Ghana. The principal instrument is a box drum (*adaka*).

Adawu: One of the music and dance pieces of the *Yewe* cult of the Anlo-Ewe of Ghana.

Adenkum: Gourd stamping tube played by the Akan of Ghana; also the name of musical type performed to the accompaniment of this instrument.

Adeudeu: A six-string lyre played in Kenya.

Adowa: Musical type of the Akan of Ghana, formerly performed at funerals, but now also performed on some ceremonial and festive occasions.

Adzobo: Drum music and dance performed by the Fon of Dahomey.

Agbadza: A recreational musical type performed by the Anlo-Ewe of Ghana.

Agbekɔ : A stylized recreational music and dance of the Anlo-Ewe of Ghana, originally performed after war to celebrate victory and enact episodes from the scene of battle by means of dance gestures.

Agutemi (akutemi): Recreational music performed by the Anlo-Ewe of Ghana.

Aho: Term in Akan for an introductory song in free rhythm.

Ajogan: Court music of the Fon of Dahomey.

Akadinda: Xylophone of twenty-two keys played in Uganda.

Akasaa: Term in Akan for a metal rattle suspended on a drum head.

Akofin: Ensemble of trumpets played at the court of kings of the Fon of Dahomey.

Akɔm: A dance of the Akan and Ga of Ghana, using intricate footwork.

Akwasidae: Memorial Sundays on which the Akan of Ghana perform music to honor the memory of ancestor chiefs.

Amadinda: Xylophone of twelve keys played in Uganda.

Amɛdzulo: A recreational musical type performed by the Ga of Ghana.

Apagya: Name of an Akan warrior organization; also, the music of this organization.

Asaadua: Recreational music performed by mixed choruses in the Akan area of Ghana.

Asafo: General name for warrior organizations of the Akan of Ghana; also, term for the music of the organizations.

Asere: Name of a royal clan in the Akan area of Ghana.

Asɔnkɔ: Name of an Akan warrior organization; also, music performed by the organization.

Asrayere: Title of a song type performed by women in the Akan area of Ghana in times of crisis.

Atamo: A small hand drum played in Ethiopia.

Atilogwu: Music and dance type performed by the Ibo of Nigeria.

Atsimewu: A long drum used in the music of the Anlo-Ewe of Ghana.

Atumpan: A drum used in Ghana for playing speech texts.

Bafumu: A religious association of the Sukuma of Tanzania.

Bagalu: A religious association of the Sukuma of Tanzania.

Bagika: A religious association of the Sukuma of Tanzania.

Bagyendanwa: A drum sacred to the Ankole of Uganda.

Bagyyangi: A religious association of the Sukuma of Tanzania.

Banunguli: A religious association of the Sukuma of Tanzania.

Banyaraja: A religious association of the Sukuma of Tanzania.

Basaji: A religious association of the Sukuma of Tanzania.

Baswezi: A religious association of the Sukuma of Tanzania.

Bayeye: A religious association of the Sukuma of Tanzania.

Begana: Name of a large lyre with eight to twelve strings, found in Ethiopia.

Bendair: Arabic drum.

Bla: Musical type performed by the Dagbani of Ghana.

Bobongo: Musical type performed by the Ekonda of Zaire.

Bokoro: One of the three principal wards or quarters into which the main section of the town of Wenchi in the Brong-Ahafo region of Ghana is divided.

Bolon: Name of a three-string arched harp, played by the Malinke of Guinea.

Bradwom: Puberty rite songs of the Akan.

Bragorɔ: Term for puberty rites performed by the Akan of Ghana. The morpheme *gorɔ* is derived from *agorɔ* play, game, while *bra* means monthly period (menses).

Bummaworowa: A wooden trumpet played by the Frafra of northern Ghana at the funerals of elderly people.

Buyeye: A traditional music club or association of the Nyamwezi of Tanzania.

Cora: A twenty-one string harp lute played in Guinea, Senegal, Gambia, and Mali in west Africa.

Dadono: A religious association of the Sukuma of Tanzania.

Damba: An Islamic festival celebrated in northern Ghana to mark the birth of Mohammed. The special music of the festival played on hourglass drums is also called *damba*.

Dea: A grand mimic war march performed by the Frafra of Ghana at the opening ceremony of the funeral of an important person.

Debtera: Professional musician and teacher in the Ethiopian Church.

Dedeleme: A recreational musical type performed by the Ewe of Ghana.

Dhikr: Literally, "remembering": technical Arabic term for the ritual mentioning of the fraternities at special gatherings.

Dipo: Puberty festival of the Adangme of Ghana.

Dzenbing: See *nasere*.

Dzera: Musical type performed by the Dagomba of Ghana.

Dzugu: Music and dance performed at funerals by the Mamprusi of Ghana.

Egungun: Ancestral cult of the Yoruba of Nigeria.

Embilta: A member of the flute family found in Ethiopia, normally made of bamboo, but also found in metal.

Endingidi: A bowed lute found in Uganda.

Entenga: Drums of the Kabaka of Uganda, played in sets of fifteen, with each drum tuned to a different pitch.

Eseni: A suite of dances performed by the Ijaw of Nigeria to the accompaniment of a set of pot drums, high-pitched, single-headed drums, and percussion sticks. Each dance has its own song and prescribed movements.

Etwie: Name of a friction drum found at the court of paramount chiefs of the Akan of Ghana. The drum is named after the leopard (*etwie*) because it imitates the snarl of this animal.

Fika ya ngoma: A ceremony performed among the Sambaa of Tanzania by the relatives of a deceased male at the first, second, third, or fourth anniversary of his death.

Fɔntɔmfrɔm: Warrior dance performed on state occasions in the Akan area of Ghana. The music is provided by an ensemble of the same name, consisting of two tall drums, the *atumpan* talking drum, and three or four small drums.

Gahu: A recreational musical type performed by the Anlo-Ewe of Ghana.

Galaganza: A musical organization of the Nyamwezi of Tanzania.

Ganga: A black African double-headed drum found in Arab north Africa.

Ghaita: An Arabic aerophone.

Golgo: A dance performed at a festival of the same name by the Frafra and Ewe of Ghana.

Gonje, goge, or goje: One-string fiddle found in the savannah belt of west Africa.

Gora: A musical bow played in South Africa by the Korana Bushman and Hottentot and adopted by the Zulu, Xhosa, and Bechuana. The tones are produced by breathing in and out on a quill which sets the string into vibration.

Griot: A praise singer.

Hari ya mɔyɔ: Name of a recreational musical association of fairly recent origin, among the Nyamwezi of Tanzania.

Hasinɔ: A designation used by the Fon of Dahomey for a person who sings long songs of praise at funerals or during festivals.

Haye: A historical song type of the Fon and Gun of Dahomey.

Husago: One of the music and dance items of the *Yewe* cult of the Anlo-Ewe of Ghana.

Ifa: A type of chant performed by the Yoruba of Nigeria.

Ijala: Chants performed by hunters of the Yoruba of Nigeria.

Itemelo: A drum played by the Sukuma of Tanzania, used for announcing the death of a chief.

Iwe: A type of chant performed by the Yoruba of Nigeria.

Iya ilu: Literally, "mother drum": name given by the Yoruba of Nigeria to the principal drum of the hourglass drum ensemble. Also used as a general term for a master drum.

Jongo: Name of a recreational music type performed by a number of different ethnic groups in northern Ghana. It consists of songs accompanied by calabash drums or ordinary drums; in some societies flutes are added to the ensemble.

Kanbonwaa: A musical type performed by the Dagomba of Ghana but modelled on the *asafo* warrior music of the Akan.

Kasomangita: A musical association found among the Nyamwezi of Tanzania.

Katanto: Drum music performed in Dahomey in connection with agricultural rites.

Kete: Music of the royal courts of Ashanti performed by a drum ensemble, sometimes with introductory pieces performed by a chorus and a flute ensemble.

Ketehoun: Musical type performed by the Fon of Dahomey.

Khalam: A plucked lute played in Senegal, Mali, and Guinea. The number of strings may range from two to five. Three-string lutes are fairly common.

Kibugander: A five-string lyre played by the Kipsigi of Kenya.

Klama: Musical type performed by the Adangme of Ghana; it has several subcategories.

Konton: One of the three principal wards or quarters into which the main section of the town of Wenchi in the Brong-Ahafo region of Ghana is divided.

Kpanligan: Name given by the Fon of Dahomey to a court minstrel who chants praise poems and historical episodes to the accompaniment of a double bell.

Kpiin iile: Term for animal horns in Gonja (spoken in Ghana).

Kple: Religious cult of the Ga of Ghana which recognizes a Supreme Being and a pantheon of lesser gods. The music of the cult is also called *kple*, and the dance, *kpledzo*.

Kpledzo: Literally, dance (*dzo*) of *kple*, a religious cult of the Ga of Ghana. The term *kpledzo* is also used for the annual festival of the gods which feature *kple* music and dance.

Krar: A six-string lyre played in Ethiopia.

Kumbeno: Term for ostinato in the Mandinka (Malinke) language spoken in Senegal, Gambia, and Guinea in the savannah belt of west Africa.

Kundum: Music and dance type performed at an annual festival of the same name by the Ahanta and the Nzema of Ghana.

Kurunku: A lament performed by the Akan of Ghana, as a solo with choral accompaniment or in the regular call-and-response form.

Kwadwomfoɔ : Name given by the Akan of Ghana to court minstrels who sing historical chants and praise poems on ceremonial occasions.

Kwella: Modern popular music of South Africa.

Kyirem: Music of one of the traditional warrior organizations of the Akan of Ghana.

Litungu: A six-string lyre found in Kenya.

Lugaya: Also *milango:* name of big drums played by the Sukuma of Tanzania.

Lunsi: Term in Dagbani (spoken in northern Ghana) for hourglass drums.

Malakat: Long metal or bamboo trumpet played in Ethiopia.

Manyanga: Musical association found among the Nyamwezi of Tanzania.

Masegera: A musical association of the Nyamwezi of Tanzania.

Masinko: One-string fiddle with diamond-shaped resonator, found in Ethiopia.

Mbeta: Flute ensemble played by the Luguru of Tanzania. Each flute plays only one note.

Mbira: Also *sansa:* a tuned idiophone consisting of wooden or metal strips arranged on a flat sounding board and mounted on a resonator.

Mbira dza Vadzimu: *Sansa* (hand piano) played in Rhodesia in connection with ancestral rituals.

Merewa: Amharic (Ethiopian) name for resonant slab of stone or wood struck with a piece of wood or a round pebble.

Miango: A team dance performed in Nigeria.

Migobo: A musical association found among the Nyamwezi of Tanzania.

Miko: Term in Kiganda (spoken in Uganda) for a system of melodic transposition which makes it possible for a tune to be played on a five-tone xylophone in five different modal forms.

Milango: See *lugaya.*

Mmaa mu: Feminine style of Akan drumming.

Mmarima mu: Masculine style of Akan drumming.

Mmobomme: Songs of exhiliaration and prayer performed by women in the Akan area in times of war or crises, or in the event of victory.

Mulizi: A flute with two finger holes played by the Bashi of Zaire.

Mvet: Idiochord zither made and played by the Fang of Cameroons.

Nagla: Flute and drum music performed at the funerals of the Kassena-Nankani of northern Ghana.

Naglagao: Music performed after the funerals of the Kassena-Nankani of northern Ghana.

Namaddu: A set of five tuned drums played by the Gwere of Uganda.

Nasera: Also *dzenbing:* funeral music of the Sisala of Ghana.

Ngodo: Dance of the Chopi of Mozambique, usually in nine to eleven movements, accompanied by a large ensemble of xylophones and percussion.

Ngoma ya mabasa: A musical category of the Sukuma of Tanzania, characterized by obscene texts.

Ngombi: A ten-string bow lute found among the Mbaka of Gabon.

Ngoni: A harp in the ancestral pantheon of the Bambara of Mali.

Nindo: Choral music type performed by the Gogo of Tanzania.

Njari: The two-manual *mbira* of the Shona-Karanga.

Nnyesoɔ : Term in Akan (spoken in Ghana) for chorus response.

Nsumankwaafoɔ : Ritual attendants at the court of the Asantehene (Ghana).

Ntahera: Ensemble of ivory horns played at the courts of paramount chiefs in the Ashanti region of Ghana.

Ntan: Literally, "bluff": name of a recreational musical type performed by the Akan of Ghana.

Ntemi: Term for chief in Sukuma language, spoken in Tanzania.

Ntimbo: A small hand drum found in Uganda.

Ntimu: Term in Akan (spoken in Ghana) for repetition.

Ntorɔ : "Spirit" transmitted by father to child in contrast with "blood" transmitted by mother to child. This concept regulates kinship among the Akan of Ghana.

Ntosoɔ : Term in Akan (spoken in Ghana) for lead singing.

Ntumu: Term used in Akan (spoken in Ghana) for interruption of chorus by a cantor.

Nyaado: A ritual drum of the Ga of Ghana.

Nyindogu: A music and dance type performed by the Dagomba of Ghana.

Nyonmo: Name given to God by the Ga of Ghana.

Obene: Stamping dance performed by the Ga of Ghana.

Obukana: A large lyre played in Kenya. It is about three-and-a-half feet long and thirty-one inches wide at the top.

Ogun: God of iron worshipped by the Yoruba of Nigeria.

Ozo: Term for a high social rank in Ibo society in Nigeria.

Ɔfre: Term in Akan for the call in a call-and-response form.

Rara: A form of chant employed by the Yoruba of Nigeria. Other types of Yoruba chant are *iwe, ifa,* and *ijala.*

Riti: Term for the one-string fiddle in Wolof, spoken in Senegal.

Sanga: A recreational musical type of the Akan of Ghana.

Sansa: See *mbira.*

Sekere: Large gourd rattle played by the Yoruba of Nigeria and the Nago of Dahomey.

Sekpele: Dance of the Lobi-Dagarti of northern Ghana, accompanied by xylophones, drums, and finger bells (metal castanets) worn by the dancers.

Senyagere: Term in Frafra (spoken in Ghana) for rattle, as well as for a song and dance type in which all performers sing and play rattles.

Sese: Also *zeze:* term for a tube fiddle in Zaire, Kenya, and Tanzania.

Seyalo: Song and dance of the Nguu of Tanzania, accompanied solely by clusters of ankle bells worn by singers.

Shantu: Gourd stamping tube played in the harems of the Hausa of Nigeria.

Sikyi: A recreational music and dance type performed by the Akan of Ghana.

Singoma: A musical association found among the Nyamwezi of Tanzania.

Siriri: A six-string lyre played in Kenya.

Sogba: One of the music and dance pieces of the *Yewe* cult of the Anlo-Ewe of Ghana.

Sowu: One of the music and dance pieces of the *Yewe* cult of the Anlo-Ewe of Ghana.

Tabale: Arabic drum.

Tegble: A heroic association in Adangme country in Ghana.

Tɛtea: A recreational musical type of the Akan of Ghana.

Tora: Musical game performed mainly by women in the Dagomba area of Ghana and the Hausa area in Nigeria.

Tsuimli: A recreational musical type performed by the Ga of Ghana.

Tuidzi: A recreational musical type performed by the Ewe of Ghana.

Tuubankpinli: A music and dance type performed by the Dagomba of Ghana.

Tuumatu: A recreational musical type performed by the Ga of Ghana.

Valiha: A tube zither played by music specialists in Malagasy.

Wombi: Chordophone played by ritual experts in Gabon.

Wumlɔnye: A drum piece in the *Yewe* cult music of the Anlo-Ewe of Ghana, featuring the *atsimewu* (a long master drum).

Yewe: A religious cult of the Anlo-Ewe of Ghana.

Yongo: Circle dance of the Builsa and Kassena-Nankani of Ghana, performed to the music of flutes, rattles, and drums.

Zeze: See *sese*.

Bibliography

ALGOA, E. J., "Songs as Historical Data: Examples from the Niger Delta," *Research Review*, V/1 (1968), 1–16.

AMES, DAVID W., "Professionals and Amateurs: The Musicians of Zaria and Obimo," *African Arts*, I/2 (1968), 40–45, 80–84.

———, "A Socio-cultural View of Hausa Musical Activity," unpublished manuscript.

———, and ANTHONY U. KING, *Glossary of Hausa Music and Its Social Context* (Evanston, 1971).

ANDERSON, LOIS, "The African Xylophone," *African Arts*, I/1 (1967), 46–49.

———, "The Interrelation of African and Arab Music. Some Preliminary Considerations," in *Essays on Music and History in Africa*, ed. K. P. Wachsmann (Evanston, 1971), 143–69.

———, *The Miko Modal System in Baganda Xylophone Music*, Ph.D. dissertation, University of California at Los Angeles, 1968.

ANDREJEWSKI, B. W., and I. M. LEWIS, *Somali Poetry* (Oxford, 1964).

ANING, B. A., *Adenkum: A Study of Akan Female Bands*, Thesis for the University of Ghana Diploma in African Music, 1964.

ANYUMBA, H. OWUOR, "The Making of a Lyre Musician," *Mila: A Biannual Newsletter of Cultural Research*, I/2 (1970), 28–33.

ATKINS, GUY, ed., *Manding: Focus on an African Civilization* (London, 1972).

BEBEY, FRANCIS, *Musique de l'Afrique* (Paris, 1969).

BEECHAM, JOHN, *Ashantee and the Gold Coast* (London, 1841).

BEIER, ULLI, *A Year of Sacred Festivals in a Yoruba Town*, ed. D. W. Macrow (Lagos, 1959).

————, *Yoruba Poetry: An Anthology of Traditional Poems* (Cambridge, 1970).

————, and BAKARE GBADAMOSI, *Yoruba Poetry* (Ibadan, 1959).

BELINGA, ENO M. S., *Littérature et Musique Populaire en Afrique Noire* (Paris, 1965).

BLACKING, JOHN, "Eight Flute Tunes from Butembo, East Belgian Congo: An Analysis in Two Parts, Musical and Physical," *African Music*, I/2 (1955), 24–52.

————, "Music and Historical Process in Vendaland," in *Essays on Music and History in Africa*, ed. K. P. Wachsmann (Evanston, 1971), 185–212.

————, "Patterns of Nsenga Kalimba Music," *African Music*, II/4 (1961), 26–43.

————, *Venda Children's Songs: A Study in Ethnomusicological Analysis* (Johannesburg, 1967).

BOAHEN, A. A., *Topics in West African History* (London 1966).

BRANDEL, ROSE, "The African Hemiola Style," *Ethnomusicology*, III/3 (1959), 106–17.

————, "Types of Melodic Movement in Central Africa," *Ethnomusicology*, VI/2 (1962), 75–87.

CARRINGTON, J. F., *Talking Drums of Africa* (London, 1949).

COPE, TREVOR, *Izibongo: Zulu Praise-Poems* (Oxford, 1968).

CORY, HANS, *African Figurines: Their Ceremonial Use in Puberty Rites in Tanganyika* (London, 1956).

————, "Ngoma Ya Shetani: An East African Native Treatment for Psychological Disorders," *Journal of the Royal Anthropological Institute*, LXVI (1936), 209.

————, *The Ntemi: The Traditional Rites in Connection with the Burial, Election, Enthronement and Magical Powers of a Sukuma Chief* (London, 1951).

————, "Some East African Native Songs," *Tanganyika Notes and Records*, IV (1937), 51–64.

————, "Tambiko or Fika," *Tanganyika Notes and Records*, LVIII (1962), 274–82.

COUPEZ, A., and MARCEL D'HERTEFELT, *La Royauté Sacrée de l'ancien Rwanda* (Tervuren, 1964).

COUPEZ, A., and T. KAMANZI, *Littérature de Cour au Rwanda* (Oxford, 1970).

COURLANDER, H., *Folk Music of Ethiopia*, album notes (Ethnic Folkways, FE 4405).

CUTTER, CHARLES H., "The Politics of Music in Mali," *African Arts*, I/3 (1968), 38–39, 74–77.

DA CRUZ, CLÉMENT, "Les Instruments de Musique du Dahomey," *Études Dahoméennes*, XII (1954), 15–36.

DOUGLAS, MARY, *The Lele of Kasai* (London, 1963).

——, "The Lele of Kasai," in *African Worlds*, ed. Daryll Forde (London, 1954), 1–24.

EDUGU, ROMANUS N., "Igodo and Ozo Festival Songs and Poems," *The Conch*, III/2 (1971), 76–88.

EGBLEWOGBE, W. Y., *Games and Songs as an Aspect of Socialisation of Children in Eweland*, M.A. thesis, University of Ghana, 1967.

ENGLAND, NICHOLAS, "Bushman Counterpoint," *Journal of the International Folk Music Council*, XIX (1967), 58–66.

ETHIOPIA, MINISTRY OF INFORMATION, *Music, Dance, and Drama in Ethiopia* (Addis Ababa, 1968).

EUBA, AKIN, "Islamic Musical Culture among the Yoruba: A Preliminary Survey," in *Essays on Music and History in Africa*, ed. K. P. Wachsmann (Evanston, 1971), 171–81.

——, "The Language of African Music," *Black Orpheus*, II/1 (1968), 44–47.

——, "Multiple Pitch Lines in Yoruba Choral Music," *Journal of the International Folk Music Council*, XIX (1967), 66–71.

——, "Music Adapts to a Changing World," *African Report*, XV/8 (1970), 24–27.

——, "New Idioms of Music—Drama among the Yoruba. An Introductory Study," *Yearbook of the International Folk Music Council*, II (1970), 92–107.

FAGG, BERNARD, "The Discovery of Multiple Rock Gongs in Nigeria," *African Music*, I/3 (1956), 6–9.

FARMER, HENRY GEORGE, "Early References to Music in the Western Sudan," *Journal of the Royal Asiatic Society* (1939), 569–80.

——, "Music," in *The Legacy of Islam*, ed. Sir Thomas Arnold and Alfred Guillaume (London, 1931), 358–59.

FOEDERMAYER, FRANZ, "The Arabian Influence in the Taureg Music," *African Music*, IV/1 (1966/67), 25–37.

FORSYTHE, REGINALD, review of William E. Ward's *Music: A Handbook for African Teachers* (London, 1939), in *Overseas Education*, XI/3 (1940), 174–75.

GAMBLE, DAVID P., *The Wolof of Senegambia* (London, 1957).

GASKIN, L. J. P., *A Select Bibliography of Music in Africa* (London, 1965).

GOODY, JACK, *Death, Property, and the Ancestors* (London, 1962).

GOURLAY, K. A., "The Making of Karimojong Cattle Songs," *Mila: A Biannual Newsletter of Cultural Research*, II/1 (1971), 34–48.

GREENBERG, J. H., *The Languages of Africa* (Bloomington, 1966).

———, *Studies in African Linguistic Classification* (New Haven, 1955).

GULLIVER, PAMELA, "Dancing Clubs of Nyasa," *Tanganyika Notes and Records*, XLI (1955), 58–59.

HALL, R. DE Z., "The Dance Societies of the Wasukuma, as seen in the Masura District," *Tanganyika Notes and Records*, I (1936), 94–96.

HARPER, PEGGY, "Dance in a Changing Society," *African Arts*, I/1 (1967), 10–13, 76–77, 79–80.

HAUSE, HELEN E., "Terms for Musical Instruments in the Sudanic Languages: A Lexicographical Inquiry," *Journal of the American Oriental Society*, Supplement 7 (1948), 1–73.

HERSKOVITS, M. J., *Dahomey*, Vol. I (Evanston, 1967).

HOLIDAY, GEOFFREY, "The Taureg of the Ahaggar," *African Music*, I/3(1956), 48–52.

HYSLOP, GRAHAM, "African Musical Instruments in Kenya," *African Music*, II/1 (1958), 31–36.

———, "More Kenya Musical Instruments," *African Music*, II/2 (1959), 24–28.

———, *Musical Instruments of Kenya*, unpublished manuscript.

———, "Some Musical Instruments of Kenya," *African Arts*, V/4 (1972), 48–55.

JEFFREYS, M. D. W., "Negro Influence on Indonesia," *African Music*, II/4 (1961), 10–16.

JOHNSON, THOMAS, "Xizambi Friction-bow Music of the Shangana-Tsonga," *African Music*, IV/4 (1970), 81–95.

JONES, A. M., *Africa and Indonesia* (Leiden, 1964).

———, *Studies in African Music* (London 1959).

KAGAME, A., *La Poesie Dynastique au Rwanda* (Brussels, 1951).

KAUFFMAN, ROBERT, *Multi-part Relationships in the Shona Music of Rhodesia*, Ph.D. dissertation, University of California at Los Angeles, 1970.

———, "Some Aspects of Aesthetics in Shona Music of Rhodesia," *Ethnomusicology*, XIII/3 (1969), 507–11.

KAZADI, PIERRE, "Congo Music: Africa's Favourite Beat," *African Report*, XVI/4 (1971), 25–27.

KEBEDE, ASHENAFI, "La Musique Sacrée de l'Eglise Orthodoxe de l'Ethiopie," in *Ethiopie: Musique de l'Eglise Copte* (Berlin, 1969).

KILSON, MARION, *Kpele Lala, Ga Religious Songs and Symbols* (Cambridge, 1971).

KING, ANTHONY, "A Report on the Use of Stone Clappers for the Accompaniment of Sacred Songs," *African Music*, II/4 (1961), 64–71.

KINNEY, SYLVIA, "Drummers in Dagbon: The Role of the Drummer in the Damba Festival," *Ethnomusicology*, XIV/2 (1970), 258–65.

KIRBY, PERCIVAL R., "The Changing Face of African Music South of the Zambezi," in *Essays on Music and History in Africa*, ed. K. P. Wachsmann (Evanston, 1971), 243–54.

———, *Musical Instruments of the Native Races of South Africa* (London, 1934).

KNIGHT, RODERICK C., *An Analytical Study of Music for the Kora, a West African Harp Lute*, M.A. thesis, University of California at Los Angeles, 1968.

KODÁLY, ZOLTÁN, "Confession," *The New Hungarian Quarterly*, III/8 (1962), 3–9.

KRIGE, E. J. and J. D., "The Lovedu of the Transvaal," in *African Worlds*, ed. Daryll Forde (London, 1954), 55–81.

KUBIK, GERHARD, "Ennanga Music," *African Music*, IV/1 (1966/67), 21–24.

———, *Mehrstimmigkeit und Tonsysteme in Zentral und Ostafrika* (Vienna, 1968).

———, "The Phenomenon of Inherent Rhythms in East and Central African Instrumental Music," *African Music*, III/1 (1962), 33–42.

———, "The Structure of Kiganda Xylophone Music," *African Music*, II/3 (1960), 6–30.

KUNENE, D. P., *Heroic Poetry of the Basotho* (London, 1971).

———, "A War Song of the Basotho," *Journal of the New African Literature and the Arts*, III (1967), 10–20.

LADZEKPO, KOBLA, "The Social Mechanics of Good Music: A Description of Dance Clubs among Anlo-Ewe Speaking Peoples of Ghana," *African Music*, V/1 (1971), 6–22.

LAYE, CAMARA, *The African Child* (Glasgow, 1959).

MACKAY, MERCEDES, "The Shantu Music of the Harems of Nigeria," *African Music*, I/2 (1955), 56–57.

MALCOLM, D. W., *Sukumaland: An African People and Their Country* (London, 1953).

MAPOMA, ISAIAH MWESA, "The Use of Folk Music among some Bemba Church Congregations in Zambia," *Yearbook of the International Folk Music Council*, I (1969), 72–88.

MBITI, J. S., *African Religions and Philosophy* (New York, 1970).

MC LEOD, NORMA, "The Status of Musical Specialists in Madagascar," *Ethnomusicology*, VIII/3 (1964), 278–89.

MENSAH, ATTA A., "The Polyphony of Gyil-gu, Kudzo and Awutu Sakumo," *Journal of the International Folk Music Council*, XIX (1967), 75–79.

MERRIAM, A. P., "The African Idiom in Music," *Journal of American Folklore,* LXXV/296 (1962), 120–30.

————, "African Music," in *Continuity and Change in African Cultures,* ed. W. R. Bascom and M. J. Herskovits (Evanston, 1958), 49–86.

————, *African Music on L.P.: An Annotated Discography* (Evanston, 1970).

————, "African Music Re-examined in the Light of New Materials from the Belgian Congo and Ruanda Urundi," *African Music Society Newsletter,* I/6 (1953), 57–64.

————, *The Anthropology of Music* (Evanston, 1964).

————, "Characteristics of African Music," *Journal of the International Folk Music Council,* II (1959), 13–19.

————, *Ekonda: Tribal Music of the Belgian Congo,* album notes (Riverside RLP-4006).

————, "Musical Instruments and Techniques of Performance among the Bashi," *Zaire,* IX/2 (1955), 121–32.

MOORE, B. T., "Categories of Traditional Liberian Songs," *Liberian Studies Journal,* II/2 (1970), 117–37.

MORRIS, H, F., *The Poetic Recitations of the Bahima of Ankole* (Oxford, 1964).

MURDOCK, G. P., *Africa, Its Peoples and Their Cultural History* (New York, 1959).

NADEL, S. F., *A Black Byzantium: The Kingdom of Nupe in Nigeria* (London, 1942; repr. 1969).

NIKIPROWETZKY, TOLI, "The Griots of Senegal and Their Instruments," *Journal of the International Folk Music Council,* XV (1963), 79–82.

NJUNGU, A. A., "The Music of My People," *African Music,* II/3 (1960), 48–50.

NKETIA, J. H. KWABENA, *African Music in Ghana* (Evanston, 1962).

————, *Drumming in Akan Communities of Ghana* (Edinburgh, 1963).

————, *Folk Songs of Ghana* (Legon, 1963).

————, *Funeral Dirges of the Akan People* (Achimota, 1955).

————, "History and the Organisation of Music in West Africa," in *Essays on Music and History in Africa,* ed. K. P. Wachsmann (Evanston, 1971), 3–25.

————, "The Hocket Technique in African Music," *Journal of the International Folk Music Council,* XIV (1962), 44–52.

————, "The Linguistic Aspect of Style," *Current Trends in Linguistics,* VII (1971), 737–47.

————, "Multi-part Organization in the Music of the Gogo of Tanzania," *Journal of the International Folk Music Council,* XIX (1967), 79–88.

————, *Music, Dance and Drama: A Review of the Performing Arts of Ghana* (Accra, 1965).

————, "The Music of Africa and African Unity," *Insight and Opinion*, V/4 (1971), 90–103.

————, *Music of the Gods*, unpublished manuscript.

————, "The Musician in Akan Society," in *The Traditional Artist in African Societies*, ed. Warren L. d'Azevedo (Bloomington, 1972).

————, "The Poetry of Akan Drums," *Black Orpheus*, II/1 (1968), 27–35.

————, "The Problem of Meaning in African Music," *Ethnomusicology*, VI/1 (1962), 1–7.

————, *The Sound Instruments of Ghana*, unpublished manuscript.

————, "Surrogate Languages of Africa," *Current Trends in Linguistics*, VII (1971), 699–732.

————, "Traditional and Contemporary Idioms of African Music," *Journal of the International Folk Music Council*, XVI (1964), 34–37.

NKHATA, A., "African Music Clubs," *African Music Society Newsletter*, I/5 (1952), 17–20.

NWOGA, D. I., "The Concept and Practice of Satire among the Igbo," *The Conch*, III/2 (1971), 30–45.

NZEWI, MEKI, "The Rhythm of Dance in Igbo Music," *The Conch*, III/2 (1971), 104–08.

OBERG, K., "The Kingdom of Ankole in Uganda," in *African Political Systems*, ed. M. Fortes and E. E. Evans-Pritchard (London, 1940), 121–62.

OGUNBA, OYIN, "The Poetic Content and Form of Yoruba Occasional Festival Songs," *African Notes*, VI/2 (1971), 10–30.

OLIVER, ROLAND, and J. D. FAGE, *A Short History of Africa* (Harmonsworth, 1962).

OPOKU, A. M., "Thoughts from the School of Music and Drama," *Okyeame*, II/1 (1964), 51–56.

OPPONG, CHRISTINE, "A Preliminary Account of the Role and Recruitment of Drummers in Dagbon," *Research Review*, VI/1 (1969), 38–51.

OTTENBERG, SIMON and PHOEBE, eds., *Cultures and Societies of Africa* (New York, 1960).

OVEN, COOTJE VAN, "Music of Sierra Leone," *African Arts*, III/4 (1970), 20–27.

OWUOR, HENRY, "Lou Song," *Black Orpheus*, X (1961), 51–56.

PANTALEONI, HEWIT, "Towards Understanding the Play of Sogo in Atsia," *Ethnomusicology*, XVI/1 (1972), 1–37.

PAQUES, VIVIANA, *Les Bambara* (Paris, 1954).

POWNE, MICHAEL, *Ethiopian Music: An Introduction* (London, 1968).

RIZZENTHELER, ROBERT and PAT, *Music of the Cameroons*, album notes (Ethnic Folkways, FE 4372).

ROUGET, GILBERT, "Court Songs and Traditional History in the Ancient Kingdoms of Porto-Novo and Abomey," in *Essays on Music and History in Africa*, ed. K. P. Wachsmann (Evanston, 1971), 27–64.

RYCROFT, DAVID, "Friction Chordophones in South Eastern Africa," *The Galpin Society Journal*, XIX (1966), 84–100.

———, "Nguni Vocal Polyphony," *Journal of the International Folk Music Council*, XIX (1967), 88–103.

———, "Zulu and Xhosa Praise Poetry and Song," *African Music*, III/1 (1962), 79–85.

SACHS, CURT, *The History of Musical Instruments* (New York, 1940).

SCHAEFFNER, ANDRÉ, *Les Kissi: Une Société Noire et Ses Instruments de Musique* (Paris, 1951).

SCHAPERA, I., *Praise-Poems of Tswana Chiefs* (London, 1965).

SCHNEIDER, MARIUS, "Tone and Tune in West African Music," *Ethnomusicology*, V/3 (1961), 204–15.

SMITH, EDNA M., "Popular Music in West Africa," *African Music*, III/1 (1962), 11–14.

SMITH, M. G., "The Hausa System of Social Status," *Africa*, XXIX (1959), 248.

———, "The Social Functions and Meaning of Hausa Praise Singing," *Africa*, XXVII/1 (1957), 26–44.

STRIDE, G. T., and CAROLINE IFEKA, eds., *Peoples and Empires of West Africa* (London, 1971).

TAIT, DAVID, *The Konkomba of Northern Ghana* (London, 1961).

THIEME, DARIUS L., "A Selected Bibliography of Periodical Articles on Music of the Native Peoples of Sub-Saharan Africa," *African Music*, III/1 (1962), 103–10.

TRACEY, ANDREW, "The Matepe Mbira Music of Rhodesia," *African Music*, IV/4 (1970), 37–61.

———, "Mbira Music of Jege A. Tapera," *African Music*, II/4 (1961), 44–63.

———, "The Tuning of Mbira Reeds," *African Music*, IV/3 (1969), 96–100.

TRACEY, HUGH, *Chopi Musicians: Their Music, Poetry, and Instruments* (London, 1948).

———, "The Mbira Class of Instruments in Rhodesia," *African Music*, IV/3 (1969), 78–95.

————, "Towards an Assessment of African Scales," *African Music*, II/1 (1958), 15–20.

TRIMINGHAM, J. SPENCER, *Islam in West Africa* (Oxford, 1959).

VANSINA, J., "The Bells of Kings," *Journal of African History*, X/2 (1969), 187–97.

————, *Oral Tradition: A Study in Historical Methodology* (London, 1965).

VIDAL, A. O., *Oriki: Praise Chants of the Yoruba*, M.A. thesis, University of California at Los Angeles, 1971.

VIDAL, TUNJI, "Oriki in Traditional Yoruba Music," *African Arts*, III/1 (1969), 56–59.

WACHSMANN, K. P., "A Century of Change in the Folk Music of an African Tribe," *Journal of the International Folk Music Council*, X (1958), 52–56.

————, "Experiments in Ugandan Music," *East Africa Journal*, III/11 (1967), 19–26.

————, "Harp Songs from Uganda," *Journal of the International Folk Music Council*, VIII (1956), 23–25.

————, "Human Migration and African Harps," *Journal of the International Folk Music Council*, XVI (1964), 84–88.

————, "Musical Instruments in the Kiganda Tradition and Their Place in the East African Scene," in *Essays on Music and History in Africa* (Evanston, 1971), 93–134.

————, "Some Speculations Concerning a Drum Chime in Baganda," *Man*, I (1965), 1–8.

————, "The Sound Instruments," in *Tribal Crafts of Uganda*, ed. Margaret Trowell and K. P. Wachsmann (London, 1958), II, 311–422.

————, "A Study of Norms in the Tribal Music of Uganda," *Ethnomusicology*, I/11 (1957), 9–15.

————, "The Transplantation of Folk Music from One Social Environment to Another," *Journal of the International Folk Music Council*, VI (1954), 41–45.

————, ed., *Essays on Music and History in Africa* (Evanston, 1971).

WARD, WILLIAM E. "Music in the Gold Coast," *Gold Coast Review*, III/2 (1927), 199–223.

WEMAN, HENRY, *African Music and Church in Africa* (Uppsala, 1960).

WILSON, MONICA, *Rituals of Kinship among the Nyakyusa* (London, 1957).

Index